BEING
UNITED
METHODIST

What It Means
Why It Matters

J. ELLSWORTH KALAS

Abingdon Press
NASHVILLE

BEING UNITED METHODIST

This book is printed on acid-free paper.

Library of Congress Cataloging-in-Publication Data has been requested.

ISBN 978-1-4267-5234-6

All scripture quotations unless noted otherwise are taken from the New Revised Standard Version of the Bible, copyright 1989, Division of Christian Education of the National Council of the Churches of Christ in the United States of America. Used by permission. All rights reserved.

Scripture quotations noted CEB are taken from the Common English Bible. Copyright © 2011 by the Common English Bible. All rights reserved. Used by permission. www.CommonEnglishBible.com.

Scripture quotations noted NIV are taken from the Holy Bible, NEW INTERNATIONAL VERSION®. Copyright © 1973, 1978, 1984 by International Bible Society. All rights reserved throughout the world. Used by permission of International Bible Society.

Scripture quotations noted KJV are taken from The Authorized (King James) Version. Rights in the Authorized Version in the United Kingdom are vested in the Crown. Reproduced by permission of the Crown's patentee, Cambridge University Press.

12 13 14 15 16 17 18 19 20 21—10 9 8 7 6 5 4 3 2 1

MANUFACTURED IN THE UNITED STATES OF AMERICA

CONTENTS

v

Contents

Chapter 1

HOW IT ALL BEGAN

O nce upon a time." That's the way our childhood stories used to begin, and something in us still wants to have just such a tidy starting place for all our stories, whether it's the story of a nation, an invention, a romance, a political movement, or a business. Or a religious denomination! It's often difficult to know the starting point for any "once upon a time." Most inventions, romances, or organizations are like human beings: there's conception, then a period of gestation before an actual coming to birth. The process is often so complicated that scholars can write dissertations on the birth of organizations, just as poets and novelists put together the pieces in a romance.

If we're to do justice to the movement called *Methodism*, then we need a scholar, a poet, a historian, and a theologian, plus some of the enthusiasm that Samuel Johnson found rather distasteful in early Methodists. Complicated as the process may be, we need to pursue it because we need to know where we've come from if we're to understand who we are and thus what we should be and what we might become. Nations need to know where they've come from and so do organizations, including religious bodies.

If I were to become quite pious, then I could say of religious bodies that it all begins with God. But I can't be satisfied with that answer because I don't think God is. Because God has created us as free moral agents, we always need to know the human element in our happenings, in the hope that perhaps we can live better with what we inherit and also do better the next time around.

For Methodists, it's a particularly complex situation because the Methodist story is difficult to categorize. Anglicans, like it or not, can locate their origins to a political power struggle between King Henry VIII and the Catholic Church. Lutherans date their origins by a climactic doctrinal issue, as do Anabaptists and the peace bodies that were part of the original Anabaptist movement. Unitarians broke away on a doctrinal issue, as did people who shaped the Pentecostal bodies. So many of these bodies and movements felt compelled to break from whatever constituted their mother church.

The Methodists, however, had no such story. There was certainly no political involvement in Methodism's birth, though we've been involved politically since then in America, England, and a variety of the new nations in other parts of the world. The people called Methodists had no desire to break from the church in which they were born, the Anglican (or Episcopal) Church, or even to reform it. Revitalize it, yes, but nothing as revolutionary as reformation. In fact, the founders of Methodism, John and Charles Wesley, remained in the Anglican Church even while some of their professional associates wished them gone. John insisted that the meeting times of the Methodist services should not compete with the times of the Anglican church services, and he rejoiced that his converts were faithful in receiving communion in their local churches. Perhaps it is no wonder that there is, in Westminster Abbey, a memorial honoring the Wesley brothers as a revered part of the Anglican story. John Wesley gladly declared that the Articles of Religion of the Church of England were hard to improve upon and passed them along to the American Methodists, in a form only slightly revised, to serve as the essence of their theological identity. The founders of Methodism didn't hate their ecclesiastical origins; they were proud of them.

There's still more to the story of Methodism's origins. Consider the night that loyal Methodists hold in particular regard as shaping their character. The Methodist movement had been in a fairly long and uncertain gestation period before this night, but the crisis came for John Wesley on May 24, 1738, when he felt his heart "strangely warmed" during a Moravian study and prayer service on Aldersgate Street in London—a place still identified by a historical marker as the birthplace of Methodism.

Now hear the story this way: the *Methodist* movement was born when an *Anglican* priest was listening to the reading of a *Lutheran* document while attending a *Moravian* gathering. No wonder, then, that Methodists are involved in almost every ecumenical, interfaith activity, and no wonder that the hymns of Charles Wesley, Methodism's cofounder, are sung in virtually every Christian body, Catholic or Protestant. Such warmhearted ecumenicity is part of Methodism's genetic code. We were born this way.

The Wesley brothers had a heart for their own Anglican Church and for the vigor of faith they found with their Moravian friends and the understanding of grace that was in Martin Luther; however, their ties went back still further. Roman Catholics were a decided minority in eighteenth-century England, often barely tolerated and certainly politically disadvantaged. But John Wesley somehow came to look beyond the usual judgments and prejudices of his time, to recognize the truths within Catholicism that belonged to all of Christendom, and to listen with love and sensitivity to the Catholics he came to know. One of Wesley's critics accused him of being "half a Papist," a derogatory term common at the time in referring to Catholics.

Wesley answered, "What if he had proved that I was a *whole* Papist?" then observed, "Is Thomas à Kempis, Mr. De Renty, Gregory Lopez gone to hell? Believe it who can."[1] And when Charles Wesley's youngest son—much against his father's wishes—became a Roman Catholic, John wrote to his young nephew, "I care not who is Head of the Church, provided you be a good Christian."

It isn't surprising, then, that so many Catholics have come to feel kinship with the Wesleys—especially John. In her delightful book, *Saint-Watching*, the Pulitzer prize-winning poet Phyllis McGinley (a devout Catholic) spent a number of pages on John Wesley as among those "saints" she found outside the Catholic Church. "I admit I am prejudiced. I love John Wesley as I love Augustine and Ignatius and Thomas Aquinas and Teresa," she writes.[2] One of my favorite biographies of John Wesley comes from John M. Todd, a Catholic layman in England. He concludes his biography, "[I] have prayed to God through him—not publicly as the Church prays through those declared to be saints—but privately as I pray for and to those who have been close to me."[3]

The point is not that the Wesley brothers were Catholic (or Eastern Orthodox, as some students seek to align them) but that they found their roots in what John called "the religion of the primitive church, of the whole church in the purest ages"—the church Wesley identified by a list of such persons as Ignatius, Polycarp, Cyprian, Chrysostom, and

Ephrem Syrus. From its birth, Methodism has known that it belongs to something bigger than itself and something older than its own birthday. This strikes me as a very wholesome, very realistic, and very Christian point of view.

So, if the Methodist movement didn't begin as reformation or as a breakaway from some mother body, what was its impetus? In a pragmatic sense, religious movements are like a commercial product: there must be a market if they are to survive. So what was Methodism's market? Clearly it was not some passing fad, a product conjured in a gathering of bright, young religious entrepreneurs as just right for this time. It's no fad when it is still present nearly three hundred years later. In America, Methodism is a force to be reckoned with for its institutions, its incomparable geographical coverage, and the way it has permeated the nation's culture and thinking. In the developing world, especially in sub-Saharan Africa and parts of Asia, it is growing numerically in sometimes spectacular fashion. True, three hundred years is not a millennium, but it is evidence that Methodism is no passing fancy. So how did it begin? What can we learn from Methodism's origins?

There was a need in England when Methodism came to birth, no doubt about that. Probably the need was no greater than in other parts of Europe and Asia, but that's another story. Methodism came to birth at a time and in a place where poverty was the norm and where most people had little reason to think it could ever be otherwise. The industrial revolution was gaining strength and villagers were changing small cities into industrial complexes. Halford Luccock and Paul Hutchinson once imagined themselves in a crowd listening to early Methodist preachers, and described it this way:

> We were not an attractive crowd. Our social lords might employ French hair-dressers and wear elaborate wigs, but our hair was likely to be matted, our scalps scrofulous, and one had only to come near us to know how seldom did we bathe. We were dirty, brutish. Most of our faces were pock-marked, for smallpox was an almost universal experience. Our clothes were ragged, made of cheap cloth and anything but in order. The pinch of underfeeding showed on many of our faces, and a sniff of the surrounding atmosphere was enough to prove that many of us were trying to make cheap gin do the work that should have been done by expensive food. And why not? Every sixth house in our city was a licensed grog-shop.[4]

Speaking of grog-shops, there was a kind of bitter humor in a sign that appeared in some of those drinking houses: "Drunk for a pence, dead-drunk for tuppence, straw free." The offer was not a sociable drink but an escape—drunkenness that seemed better than the reality of daily life that so much of the populace knew. And when one had drunk himself into oblivion, there was straw in a corner where the body could lie until some measure of pained sobriety returned.

In such a time of human need, some of us would say that the church is the hope. Well, it *should* be. But in eighteenth-century England, the church seems often to have been more a part of the problem than of any solution. Certainly it was doing little or nothing for the kind of people Luccock and Hutchinson described. John Wesley put it with a directness that makes him sound like Martin Luther: "Nine tenths of the men in England have no more religion than horses, and perish through total contempt of it."

It's the *contempt* factor that was the worst. There's hope in the midst of a plague if people respect the physicians, and possibilities in times of war or social upheaval if the citizens have reason to trust their political leaders, and hope for the spiritual recovery of a nation if there are saints and prophets in the land. But England was a nation with a state church, and when church and state are one, both are in danger. Samuel Johnson put it sharply: "No man can now be a bishop for his learning and piety. His only chance of promotion is his being connected with someone who has parliamentary interest." Because bishops gained their office by way of king and parliament, they tended to be men who knew on which side their bread was buttered and who, therefore, worried more about keeping the favor of those in power than in meeting the spiritual and daily needs of those in their care.

Bishops of such a character were likely, in turn, to appoint persons like themselves who looked only for advancement. Perhaps the worst crime in this regard was the rather common practice of appointing clergy to several parishes with comfortable income, with these clergy then hiring curates—at a very low salary, often less than a footman earned—who did the actual work of the parish while the appointed clergy appeared rarely, if at all. Nevertheless, a hunger for God remained. One marvels that, even in the worst of times, the sheep look up, hoping to be fed, because they know instinctively that their hunger ought to be met. Thus, in the hundreds of country parsonages, there was a constant demand for devotional literature. Many good, even if ill-trained, clergy served these churches with commendable earnestness.

One should not conclude that all of the bishops and archbishops were as bad as popular history portrays them. Mind you, the system was conducive to abuse and most of us humans are susceptible to such attractions—and all the more so when power comes with it because power is the ultimate intoxicant. Nevertheless, there was enough goodness left in the Anglican Church of the eighteenth century that it could produce John and Charles Wesley and George Whitefield and John Newton, William Wilberforce, and a host of less memorable souls. There was enough common sense in the Anglican Church that its leaders did not expel the Wesley brothers, even though it must have been clear that their Methodist Societies were, in so many ways, in direct competition to the Anglican establishment. I can hardly imagine contemporary United Methodism allowing any of its ordained clergy to build independent meeting houses in communities where a United Methodist Church already exists, as John and Charles Wesley and their followers did. In this respect, perhaps the state church system was a blessing. Because the church didn't depend on its members for financial security, its leaders weren't as troubled about the competition the Methodist movement provided. Otherwise they might have dealt more directly with John and Charles, and the Methodist movement might never have come to pass.

Perhaps we should put the matter quite simply and baldly and say that there was a need and that Methodism somehow met it. The need was deep and profound. There was financial poverty and social inequity, but these had always existed. The industrial revolution was intensifying these issues, however, and perhaps robbing people of some of the beauty and tranquility of nature that had previously made the poverty and social disorder easier to endure. There was a kind of endemic hopelessness; one could run from it by way of the grog shop and a stupefaction of sensibility, but always there came a time of waking up again, with the hopelessness still there.

Into that world a preacher came, John Wesley, as logical as a college debater, as earnest as a primary teacher, and as impassioned as a salesman who thinks this is his last prospect. And with him, music came: words by his brother Charles and tunes wherever they might be found but with a message that insisted there was God, there was going to be a tomorrow, and that one must live in a way that deserved tomorrow and intended to do something about it.

Perhaps, in the purposes of God and in the sometimes strange configuring of events that we call history, it was *time*. Is it possible that circumstances have to reach a certain degree of hopelessness before hope can flex its holy muscles? The classic biblical incident tells of a time when "humanity had become thoroughly evil on the earth and that every idea their minds thought up was always completely evil"; so much so that God regretted that he had made human beings on the earth (Genesis 6:5-6, CEB). And then there was Noah: "the LORD approved of him." He was "a moral and exemplary man; he walked with God" (Genesis 6:8-9, CEB). How comes a Noah, when everyone else is "thoroughly evil"? And how comes a revival within a church that is corrupted by its system and stagnant in most of its pulpits?

We need to know because our times have a peculiar crisis quality. We have lost our moral moorings because our generation is no longer sure that there is a moral compass. Something in our economics is slowly killing the American dream so that opportunity for all is steadily becoming increasing privilege for an ever-smaller number. Our culture has become like our eating habits—a drive-by, eat-on-the-run, get the quickest kick we can from our music, our dance, our sports, our books (what are books?), our communication.

As for religion, our yearning is still there. We still look up, hoping to be fed. But we look for spirituality, which remains comfortably undefined, and hear little of daily responsibility. We're hell-bent in a search for something new, appealing, clever, culturally competitive; who cares if it is only two inches deep and a mile wide? We know we need some saints, but we're not sure we'd recognize them if such should appear.

Is it possible that the movement called Methodism could once again rise to the need, as it did in eighteenth-century England and nineteenth-century America? Is there any place in twenty-first-century Methodism for the kind of renewal that came in eighteenth-century Anglicanism?

Perhaps the past can tell us what to do in the present so that we can walk with God into a redeemed and redeeming future. It's worth a try.

Chapter 2

A VILLAGE THAT MADE A
DIFFERENCE

Even with England's admirable system of public trans-
portation, it isn't easy to get to Epworth, in
Lincolnshire. Epworth is a modest village with a population
just under 3,500. Yet thousands of people from every part of
the world make their own kind of pilgrimage there every
year. Except for some biblical towns, probably no community of similar size has given its name to a greater variety of
organizations, spread over a wider geography than has
Epworth. In the United States, there are children's homes and
retirement communities, retreat centers and summer camps,
and hundreds of churches that have taken the name. For

some forty years at the end of the nineteenth century and the beginning of the twentieth, it was the name of the most vigorous youth movement in the United States and Canada, the Epworth League.

When Samuel Wesley came to Epworth in 1695 to become rector of its little Anglican church, he was a person of grand imaginings; he came eventually to see himself as the Poet of the Isle of Axholme, but he could never have imagined that people would be discussing him and his family more than three centuries later and that they would come to the village and stand thoughtfully by his burial place. I doubt that he intended to stay there for nearly forty years, as he did. Samuel loved to write, which he did reasonably well, and hoped to establish himself and augment his income by writing. But his greatest achievement, as it turned out, was in the family he and his wife Susanna raised, particularly their sons John and Charles, two of the nineteen children born to their marriage during its first twenty-one years.

Both Samuel and Susanna came from good stock, and both had minds of their own. Both descended from two generations of Puritan nonconformist preachers, and both chose to return to the state church, the Anglican Church. Nevertheless, the Puritan passion for vital piety never left either Samuel or Susanna. Where many rectors in the state church too readily saw their work as a means of income and little more, Samuel sought to bring the people of his parish to personal faith and commitment. "The inward witness, son, the inward witness—this is the proof, the strongest proof, of Christianity," he told son John in his dying hours. The "inward witness" of personal religious experience became the essence of the Methodist movement. In the same waning time of his life, Samuel told Charles, "Charles, be steady; the Christian faith will surely revive in these kingdoms. You shall see it, though I shall not." Samuel's words sound like those of a prophet. Charles not only saw such a revival of Christianity in the British Isles but he and John led the way.

The thought of nineteen births in twenty-one years is almost unimaginable in our culture, especially when we think of its being without the aid of modern pain relievers or anesthesia, but, no doubt, Susanna was emotionally prepared for such a life. When someone asked her father, Dr. Annesley, a revered scholar, the size of his family, he answered that it was either two dozen or a quarter of a hundred. With that many children, one might lose count! As it happens, Susanna was number twenty-five, so it mattered to her.

Ten of Samuel and Susanna's children died in infancy, a percentage not uncommon in that world and time. Susanna raised the children with a strictness that the postmodern world would critique. She taught each child to cry quietly by its first birthday. It was a disciplined household but a loving one. The children learned early that "they might have nothing they cried for, and instructed to speak handsomely for what they wanted."[1] Apparently, even in that day, some people looked upon Susanna's methods as severe. When John was a young man and asked his mother to tell of her beliefs about raising a family, she wrote, "In the esteem of the world they pass for kind and indulgent, whom I call cruel parents, who permit their children to get habits which they know must be afterwards broken."[2]

She emphasized respecting the rights of others. Not only were the children forbidden to take God's name in vain but they were also to treat each other's names with respect, always adding "brother" or "sister" to the proper name when calling a sibling. Each child's personal property was "inviolably preserved," and they did not "invade the property of another in the smallest matter, though it were but of the value of a farthing, or a pin." The promises they made to each other were to be "strictly observed."

Susanna home-schooled the children. In a world where few female children had the privilege of education, Susanna insisted, "That no girl be taught to work till she can read very well, and then that she be kept to her work with the same application." "Putting children to learn sewing before they can read perfectly is the very reason why so few women can read fit to be heard, and never to be well understood."[3]

Some critics suggest that Susanna did her daughters no favor in educating them so far beyond their peers because it meant that they were quite unlikely to marry a man of comparable education and intelligence. No doubt, some of the daughters married unhappily—partly, it appears, because of their father's meddling. I'd certainly hesitate to say that a person should leave a mind undeveloped because, with learning and intelligence, he or she might feel out of place in a daily environment. A person with capacity to learn might feel out of place in his or her surroundings whether educated or not, simply by reason of an innate taste for more than is commonly available.

Mehetabel—"Hetty" to her siblings and parents—was probably the brightest of the girls and perhaps the one who suffered most from the disappointments of marriage. The *Oxford Dictionary of Quotations* carries two excerpts from her poetry, including two poignant lines written "To an Infant Expiring the Second Day of Its Birth": "Transient luster, beauteous clay, Smiling wonder of a day."[4] Anyone reading about the Wesley daughters is likely to think also of another Anglican parsonage, Haworth, where the more famous daughters of Patrick Bronte, Charlotte, Emily, and Anne, lived out their creativity a century later. G. Elsie Harrison, biographer of John Wesley, felt that the Wesley daughters deserved comparison with the Brontes.

Philosophies of child-rearing have their own pendulum swing from generation to generation, so it's probably wise to comment cautiously on Susanna Wesley's methods. It's especially important to remember that particular words and concepts have different meanings from one generation to another. Susanna may sound extreme when she says that she sought to break a child's will early. Certainly it can be said that the Wesley children were in no way intimidated by her methods; to the contrary, both the boys and the girls were strong-spirited with vigorous minds and a sense of social responsibility. None of their adult correspondence suggests that they resented their early schooling or their mother's methods; rather, John sought his mother's counsel. As Maldwyn Edwards wrote in the mid-twentieth century, "The tree is known by its fruits, and no final judgment on Susanna's method can overlook the results that she obtained."[5]

There was no question in son John's mind. He wrote of her, "Take her for all and in all, I do not believe that any human being ever brought into the world and carried through it a larger portion of original goodness than my dear mother. Everyone who knew her loved her, for she seemed to be made to be happy herself, and to make everyone happy within her little sphere."[6]

Scholarship was native to the Wesley family and books and learning were key elements in the Epworth household. Samuel was accomplished in several languages, and his love for detail and minutiae gave him joy in research. There was little opportunity in the Epworth parish for stimulating conversation; one wonders how far Samuel's interests might have escaped the people to whom he was preaching. He

spent the last thirty years of his life writing a commentary on
the Old Testament book of Job, in Latin. During the course
of his writing, he suffered paralysis of his writing hand but
learned to write with the other. As he reported in a letter to
a friend, "though I have already lost the use of one hand in
the service, yet, I thank God, *non defecit altera*, and I begin
to put it to school this day to learn to write, in order to help
its lame brother."[7] Samuel died before his book was published, but he had dedicated the book to Queen Caroline, so
son John delivered a copy to the queen. She received him
kindly, said that the book was "very prettily bound," then
laid it on a window seat without opening it.

Samuel took his religion seriously, as he did his scholarship; more seriously than the little island community
desired and, as some biographies have noted, Samuel was
not always a tactful man. The parish, in return, made their
feelings clear. In 1702 two-thirds of the parsonage was
destroyed by fire, and two years later, another fire
destroyed all of Wesley's flax crop. The next year some of
his enemies maimed several of his farm animals and his
dog. Then, in February 1709, apparently some Epworth
ruffians set fire again to the rectory. It appeared that everyone had escaped when someone heard a cry from the nursery where five-year-old John was standing at a window.
Neighbors made a human ladder and brought the boy
down before the roof collapsed inward. In the midst of the
ashes, Samuel's spirit was unbroken. "Come, neighbors,"

he shouted, "let us kneel down! Let us give thanks to God! He has given me all my eight children, let the house go, I am rich enough."

The event was seminal in John Wesley's life. He would ever after see himself as "a brand plucked from the burning"; he returns to that phrase several times in his journal when he passes through circumstances and decisions that might hurt his walk with God. As for his mother, John's narrow escape underlined a conviction she had recorded nearly two years before: "I do intend to be more particularly careful with the soul of this child than ever I have been; that I may instill into his mind the principles of true religion and virtue." She succeeded, no doubt about that.

When you read excerpts from Susanna's letters and ponder her strength of person, you can't help wondering what she might have done in a later century. I suspect she might have become a corporate executive at some level or another, or perhaps president of a college or university. Samuel farmed, as did most village rectors at the time, but never well, and although his income was moderately good, he was not a good manager. Susanna once wrote that she had learned that Samuel was not "fit for business. My own experience hath since convinced me that he is one of those who, our Saviour saith, are not so wise in their generation as the children of this world."[8] But Susanna made the most of managing the household; single-handed for periods when Samuel was in debtors' prison and, on other occasions, when risen waters and a marsh around Epworth kept him in London for months at a time.

During one of those periods, people from the parish began attending Sunday evening prayers in the rectory under Susanna's leadership. The attendance grew remarkably. When Samuel heard what was happening, he wrote her that she was violating teachings of the church and of Saint Paul. She replied with a report of how much good was happening and that she would not stop unless Samuel specifically commanded her to do so. He apparently decided not to go that far, a decision that clearly was wise.

It seems that the marriage was often strained. Samuel left for an extended period when during evening prayers Susanna refused to say "Amen" to Samuel's prayer for King William III. Samuel insisted that, if Susanna could not agree with him politically and support his prayer for King William, then they must part; if they had two kings, they must have two beds, so he left for London. Eventually he regretted his action and returned in time for the birth of Anne, and some time after that for John's conception. But, as Susanna wrote to John during his days at Oxford, "It is an unhappiness peculiar to our family that your father and I never think alike on anything." Daughter Emily said that her father had an "unaccountable love of discord." I think there are such people, but of course, I can't judge if this was true of Samuel Wesley. It is certain, however, that Samuel and Susanna were both very strong personalities and that living in accord must at times have strained both of them.

In spite of years when the people of the Epworth parish made life difficult for Samuel, he slogged on and seemed eventually to win their respect, staying there until his death. He wrote to Samuel Jr. in February 1733, that attendance at the Communion service had grown from twenty to more than a hundred and that, after nearly forty years of ministry, his people "grew better."[9] I honor Samuel for having a pastor's heart, not only in his desire that the congregation should increase in godliness but also in his unceasing confidence that they would do so, a confidence that kept him at his task for so many years in what most would have seen as an unpromising field. In this he can be an encouragement and an example to vast numbers of pastors and priests who serve in hidden and apparently unfruitful places.

Late in his life, John Wesley wrote to Adam Clarke, Methodism's rising young scholar, "If I were to write my own life, I should begin it before I was born."[10] I suppose this is a proper statement for any of us because all of us are products not only of our physical parentage but also of the geographical, economic, and political factors as well. The common experience was especially significant for John Wesley for a number of reasons. It isn't insignificant that John, the only child with two names, got his names from two older brothers, John and Benjamin, who died in infancy. He was endowed with a double or triple obligation from the hour of his naming. In addition, the political climate before John's birth—that is, the controversy over King William III—agitated his parents so dramatically as to set a philosophical temper in their home.

One realizes that both parents were strong personalities. G. Elsie Harrison, in a biography of John written in the first third of the twentieth century, titled her work *Son to Susanna*, indicating her conviction that Susanna—and John's sisters and later several women—were dominant influences in his life. But John was Samuel's son, too. Maldwyn Edwards notes that both John and Charles "inherited their father's trait of physical and moral courage. . . . Neither allowed any obstacles to daunt them, nor any adversities to wear down their spirits."[11] When John tells his fledgling preachers, "Always to look a mob in the eye,"[12] he is counseling them from his own indomitable readiness to dare rotten eggs, spoiled vegetables, and even bricks and stones. In this he reflected the tiny rector of Epworth who stayed on in a parish where the ruffians tried to threaten and burn him out, and in forty years, Samuel finally won the battle.

Both Samuel and Susanna gave their children a love for learning. It isn't surprising that Samuel was a scholar; he was part of an extended era when clergy were expected to be the most learned people in their communities. Susanna was, in her own way, Samuel's intellectual equal: not the linguistic scholar he was but with a sound grasp of Christian doctrine and a particular gift for applying her knowledge in practical judgment. Harrison isn't inappropriate when she refers to Susanna and her "nursery of scholars," a setting in which she spent six hours daily in home-schooling. It is no doubt true that John Wesley would never meet better educated women than his own sisters.

Without a doubt this home experience affected Wesley's attitude toward the role of women in the church. He gave them positions of authority in administration without hesitancy and sought the counsel of women quite naturally. As Elsie Harrison put it, "John Wesley, in the work of the revival in England, was to give a special place of importance to women and to pay them the compliment of equality."[13] In this he was centuries ahead of his time.

John and Charles's grandfathers and great grandfathers were both dissenters from the Anglican Church, but both John and Charles remained in the established church. Yet, in a very wonderful way, both kept something of the dissenter in their souls, and John, in particular, dared to bend the system without breaking his relationship with it. To the day of his death, he was a holy gadfly intent on renewing the church that he loved—but that he loved with a passion to see it become what it professed to be.

When Susanna Wesley was near death, the children gathered around her, and John began to sing and the sisters joined him. Susanna had said, "As soon as I am released, children, sing a psalm of praise to God." John loved, in later years, to say of his Methodists, that they "died well." Susanna gave him a proper example. Her last, glad words were, "My dear Saviour! Are you come to help me in my extremity at last?"[14]

Such was Methodism's heritage in the often-swampland of eighteenth-century Epworth. It didn't know it when it was in the process, but Epworth was a village that made a difference in human history. And it continues to do so nearly three hundred years later.

Chapter 3

HOW TO BE EXCLUSIVELY
INCLUSIVE

If you listen carefully to Jesus, then you realize that no one ever opened a wider door of hope and love to the human race. As you continue to listen, you understand that the door is so narrow that you must strip yourself to life's core in order to pass through.

"Come to me," Jesus said, "all you that are weary and are carrying heavy burdens, and I will give you rest. Take my yoke upon you, and learn from me; for I am gentle and humble in heart, and you will find rest for your souls. For my yoke is easy, and my burden is light" (Matthew 11:28-30). No invitation could be more inclusive, more welcoming.

Those who customarily feel most shut out are told that there are no barriers here; the very issues that weigh against them elsewhere are votes in their favor in Christ's kingdom.

In the Sermon on the Mount Jesus sounds a very different note. "Enter through the narrow gate; for the gate is wide and the road is easy that leads to destruction, and there are many who take it. For the gate is narrow and the road is hard that leads to life, and there are few who find it" (Matthew 7:13-14). When some apparently sincere people volunteered to join his team, Jesus abruptly discouraged them. To a scribe—the kind of trained religious leader that would have added some muscle to Jesus' generally ill-prepared group—Jesus warned that there was no future with him: "Foxes have holes, and birds of the air have nests; but the Son of Man has nowhere to lay his head" (Matthew 8:20). So too was the case with a man who was already a disciple but who wanted now to join the inner circle. When he asked permission to bury his father, Jesus quickly advised him that his interest level wasn't enough for true discipleship (Matthew 8:21-22).

The point was clear, even if confusing. Jesus' invitation was all-inclusive; "whosoever will may come." Those who came found that if they were to stay, to go with Jesus all the way, they must be dead in earnest.

The Methodist movement caught this inclusive-exclusive policy better than any expression of Christianity before or since. Theologically, early Methodism was fiercely inclusive.

I use the word "fiercely" intentionally, with no sense of exaggeration. As Wesley preached out of doors, in the fields and in the village centers, his location itself indicated that he wanted anybody and everybody. The conventional church or meeting house waited for persons to come; Wesley and his fellow preachers went where the people were. In a sense, he sought no converts. There were no cards to sign (a high percentage of his listeners couldn't write), no altar at which converts could kneel. He invited any who were interested to visit a group for further inquiry. The only requirement was that they desired to "flee from the wrath to come." That is, that they wanted to escape the fatal judgment.

Wesley's theological position was vigorously opposed to the Calvinism which was so strong at the time. The Calvinists argued that a person could be saved only if he or she belonged to "the elect"—that is, those whom God had already chosen. The Wesley brothers considered this a "damnable doctrine." In a typical Methodist hymn, Charles Wesley taught the Methodists to sing,

> Help us thy mercy to extol,
> Immense, unfathomed, *unconfined*;
> To praise the Lamb who died for *all*,
> The *general* Savior of mankind.
> . . . .
> The *world* he suffered to redeem;
> For *all* he hath the atonement made;
> For *those that will not come to him*,
> The ransom of his life was paid.
> ("Father, Whose Love Everlasting," 1741)

I have italicized words in this hymn as the British theologian Philip S. Watson did. Watson explained that he did so because "we may suspect it was written with a consciously anti-Calvinist intent."[1] Charles Wesley wanted every lost soul to know that the door was open wide, wide enough for the worst sinner. Christ had died even for "those that will not come to him." Wesley considered himself as part of the group for whom the gospel door must be mercifully wide. He wrote his hymns with a fine sense of his own need of a Savior. Most of us would see Charles as a person of exemplary conduct, but he saw himself as a person who needed a Savior as badly as the person maligned and condemned by common society. He was confident of the same saving grace. This was a theology that embraced all, including those who might not want to be identified as being in need—though, of course, they would eventually have to admit their need, else they wouldn't accept the gracious offer.

Jesus said the kingdom of God was like a farmer who sowed his seed broadcast—some on the roadway, some on hard soil, some in the midst of weeds, and some in good soil. The farmer wasn't scientific about it; in truth, he seemed quite reckless and wasteful as if every kind of soil deserved a chance. The Methodists were like that. They didn't seek out "good prospects" or "interested people." As I have already indicated, they preached in the public square or open fields or mine entrances. Nobody was too poor, too ignorant, too indifferent, or too lost to be outside the range of their seeking and caring. They preached in a rigidly stratified social culture and insisted that everyone, regardless of their rank or learning or wealth, was in need of a Savior, and that this Savior welcomed everyone at the same wide-open door.

When we come to the story of Methodism in America, we will see that this radically inclusive approach was made to order for the American dream (indeed, in a sense, it probably helped to shape the dream) and that, as long as the Methodists reached out with such democratic abandon, they grew. More often than not, those who came to America were people who were looking for a chance that the more stratified social structure of Europe didn't offer. Many of America's first settlers were Puritans who saw themselves as elect, but the immigrants who later followed in droves had no such estimate of themselves. Thus the Methodist message of "whosoever will" fit their social, economic, and spiritual status exactly.

John and Charles Wesley and the group that grew around them saw something else in the common soil of the human soul. They believed that the hunger in every soul was such that they could make grand commitments to Christ and that it was theirs to do. At this point, the system showed its exclusive side. It was easy to get in, but it was hard to stay. The door was wide: "all who would flee from the wrath to come." Then it became demanding because the goal was perfection. Methodism was in the business of making saints. If you stayed around, you discovered that you were becoming, of all things, *holy*. And this is exclusive territory. The air is thin up here!

Let me excerpt some lines from John Wesley's counsel. For those who wanted God to work in their lives, Wesley urged that they "fly from all sin as from the face of a serpent; carefully avoid every evil word and work; yea, abstain from all appearance of evil. . . . Be zealous of good works, of works of piety as well as works of mercy; family prayer, and crying to God in secret. Fast in secret and 'your Father which seeth in secret, he will reward you openly.' 'Search the Scriptures'; hear them in public, read them in private, and meditate therein. At every opportunity, be a partaker of the Lord's Supper. . . . Let your conversation be with the children of God; and see that it 'be in grace, seasoned with salt.' As ye have time, do good unto all men; to their souls and to their bodies. . . . Deny yourselves every pleasure which does not prepare you for taking pleasure in God, and willingly embrace every means of drawing near to God, though it be a cross, though it be grievous to flesh and blood. Thus when you have redemption in the blood of Christ, you will 'go on to perfection.' "[2]

He had a *method* for this. The Methodists didn't exhort in generalities; they provided a plan and a way. It had to do with social religion. John Wesley had little, if any, confidence in private piety; he believed that we need one another and that it is important that we come together to strengthen, confirm, and correct one another. Thus it was that he set up a system rather like what he and Charles and their fellow Oxford students had known in their student days, a system in which they watched over one another's souls.

In November 1738, when John Wesley's own Aldersgate experience was still very fresh, the experience began to take form as a movement, though I doubt that Wesley had such intentions at that point. Nearly thirty years later, Wesley recalled the story for his annual conference of Methodist preachers. He recalled that several persons came to him in London, asking him to "advise and pray with them." Wesley answered, "If you will meet on Thursday night, I will help you as well as I can." The group increased into hundreds; these were hungry souls, who took their new faith seriously. Wesley continued, "The case was afterward the same at Bristol, Kingswood, Newcastle, and many other parts of England, Scotland, and Ireland."[3]

This was the beginning of what came to be known as Methodist societies. In a sense, they were similar to other such groups of Quakers and Moravians. The state church, the Church of England, was at the time more a formality than a living commitment, and it was groups such as these in numbers of dissenting bodies that met the needs of earnest believers, people who wanted a transforming reality in their lives.

The Methodist societies grew much more dramatically, however, than did the others, and the difference was in the discipline and structure that the Wesley brothers provided for their societies. John Wesley said that a Methodist society would consist of "a company of men [Wesley used the term generically; women were part of the program from the beginning] having the form and seeking the power of godliness, united in order to pray together, to receive the word of exhortation, and to watch over one another in love, that they may help each other to work out their own salvation."[4] I wonder what would happen in contemporary Methodism if each congregation, or indeed each adult or youth group, were to make such a statement their reason for existence: seeking the power of godliness, united to pray together, receive exhortation, and to watch over one another in love, with the goal of helping one another work out their salvation. Does the language seem quaint? Perhaps it is not so quaint as it is clear, basic, and demanding. Perhaps we wish it were quaint so we could avoid its demands.

Even as I write I think I can hear someone say, "If we dared to institute such a standard, we would soon lose two-thirds of our group, if not more." Here it is that the *inclusive* invitation becomes *exclusive*. Wesley wasn't fascinated by statistics. Mind you, he watched over every soul with singular concern, but he found no solace in sheer numbers. So he pared away at the rolls, seeking always for excellence in living and high levels of commitment.

The secret was in what we would now call "the small group" program; Wesley called it the "class meeting." He divided the societies into groups of about twelve with a leader responsible for the group. The leader conducted the weekly meeting which was the occasion for inquiring into the state of soul of each person in the group. He was an exhorter in both word and spirit, encouraging the faltering, stimulating the marginal, and correcting the indifferent. The goal was holiness of life. Those first Methodists believed it was worth pursuing, and they realized it was not easy to attain.

The format for the weekly meetings was not glamorous nor was it for the faint of heart. There was an opening hymn; with Charles producing new poems almost daily, there was never a shortage of something to sing. Then a season of prayer and then Bible teaching from the leader. Whatever the content of the lesson, it was inclined to sound like an exhortation because, whatever was studied, the ultimate goal was a deeper, more consistent Christian walk. Then came the time of soul-searching.

In our day, many would probably see this activity as group therapy. It was much more than that, and it was by all odds a test in earnestness. The basic question: "How is it, brother/sister, with your soul?" The first answer might easily be general and predictable, but the leader rarely left matters at that level. He would probe away like a dental technician on the hunt for a cavity. The leader knew the group and they knew one another, so he would inquire at how the individual was doing with what the Bible would call his or her "besetting sin." Vague answers weren't sufficient.

Nevertheless, members were allowed to keep private what they felt should be private, and at its best, the group was caring and supportive. Obviously, it wasn't a perfect system, and if I know human nature, leaders were probably ineffective at times and unduly aggressive at other times. I would presume that fellow members of a class sometimes divulged private matters outside the meeting, but the general tenor was wholesome and nurturing.

By rule, if a person was absent from three consecutive meetings, he or she lost the "ticket" that was necessary for admission to the quarterly meetings of the society. Clearly, there were no Easter/Christmas members in early Methodism. The movement was not a membership to be listed in one's obituary; it was a way of life. It was an honor and an achievement, but the Methodists prized it primarily because, by way of the class meeting, they hoped to make their calling and election sure.

For a time, the Methodists also had a small group known as "bands." These were usually made up of persons of one sex which made it easier for discussion of more intimate matters. The bands never gained the prominence or the practical effectiveness of the class meetings, and over time, they ceased to exist. The class meetings, on the other hand, were probably as important to the growth and quality of Methodism as its preaching and its singing, and in some ways, even more important.

Eventually, however, the class meetings fell by the way-side in the British Isles and later in America. Perhaps the reason was simply the principle by which all methods and systems have their day, then lose their appeal. Perhaps new generations found it hard to maintain what had meant so much to their forebears. Perhaps, too, the rise of the Sunday school movement and later of youth programming filled some of the purposes of the class meeting. I am convinced that some adult classes, led by sensitive and capable persons, got some of the nurturing quality of the class meetings, and so too with youth groups in instances of particularly effective leadership.

Several times within the last sixty years, Methodism in America has tried to revive the class meeting via the "small group" movement, but these efforts have rarely taken hold in any strong or continuing way. Perhaps this failure is because the modern and postmodern small group efforts have been seen as programs for denominational growth, whereas, in the early days of Methodism, the goal was spiritual nurture, a method for leading believers into a vital Christian life. It seems clear that we will not bring ourselves under the kind of discipline that the class meetings espoused unless the goal is attractive enough to merit the discipline. That is, one must believe that the Christian life is worth the trouble. The early Methodists had no doubt about this. I fear the present generation is not so deeply convinced.

When you and I read of the demanding quality of the class meetings and the strict discipline of the Methodist societies, we may see our spiritual ancestors as a terribly earnest lot, so set on heaven that earth was a burden. There's no doubt that they were terribly in earnest; this was part of their DNA. But it was no burden. The early Methodists were among the happiest of souls. As John Wesley famously said, "Sour godliness is the devil's religion."[5] When seekers and critics alike asked Wesley, "Who is a Methodist," an early part of his answer ran like this: "God is the joy of his heart, the desire of his soul. . . . He is therefore happy in God, yea, always happy." Having found redemption in Christ, "he cannot but rejoice, whenever he looks back on the horrible pit out of which he has been delivered . . . [and] whenever he looks on the state wherein he now is 'being justified freely, and having peace with God through our Lord Jesus Christ.' "[6]

It proved to be so for those who gave themselves fully to this new faith. They were a people who saw a door as wide as the love of God, open to any who would choose to enter, but with a path so narrow in its demands that only the truly convinced would pay the full price. It was a way as inclusive as the love of God and as exclusive as the readiness of the human heart to follow on. This was Methodism as its founders dreamed and as they expected it to be. Like most great dreams, it is difficult for succeeding generations to perceive, to understand fully, and to live out effectively.

Is such earnestness possible in our day? I'm confident that we humans are as God-hungry as ever. But our lives are complicated. When we read that every sixth house in London was a grog shop, we know that distraction was near at hand. At least in their day, they had to walk out of the house to give in to the distraction. In our day, the distraction is in several rooms of the house, with ever-larger screens. And worse, now it is in hand, like a super-extension of nature's arm. We'll have to care enough to flee from some of our distractions if we're to get an eye and ear and heart intent upon God.

The human soul still wants more of the Spirit of God. Perhaps we need simply to say more clearly, "Here is the widest of doors; everyone is welcome"—and then to say, "Here is the most demanding—and *exciting*—of ways. Welcome to the challenge!"

Chapter 4

A PEOPLE OF

HEAD AND HEART

For six years of my pastoral ministry, I had the privilege of looking into the heart of Methodism each time I stood up to preach. The First United Methodist Church in Green Bay, Wisconsin, is beautiful in both its English Gothic architecture and its stained glass windows. Those windows celebrate the traditional symbols of Christianity, the kind of symbols one might see in some form in almost any Christian church. But the window facing the preacher as he or she steps into the pulpit on any given occasion is typically American and typically Methodist. *Saddlebags*.

Some might object for aesthetic reasons to saddlebags as a subject for stained glass art. Others might think the form inappropriate for a Christian symbol. I saw the window as the essence of what it means to be a Methodist preacher and as the heart of the Methodist attitude toward life and the gospel.

At this point, I must confess that I don't know what the artist had in mind in choosing saddlebags for what, in many classic churches, is one of the two most significant windows in the church. But for me, the saddlebags said two things. They testified to the heart of Methodism in the days when its preachers invaded the new frontier with a passion to win the nation for Jesus Christ. No one would dare to live as those preachers lived in their everyday struggle with the elements and often with unwelcoming communities unless they were heart-driven. They may have been fools, but they weren't soft. They may have forsaken common sense in their desire to plant churches wherever they found a scattering of houses, but they weren't short of passion. This was a people of the heart.

What did they have in their saddlebags? *Books.* The preacher's Bible and notebook, of course, but also books to sell and to give away. The Methodist Publishing House, established in 1789, provided its frontier preachers with books. Someone in early American Methodism understood that, while conversion might seem to begin in the heart, it would have to be sustained in the mind if the convert and the movement were to last beyond the first blush of excitement. No one can estimate how many frontier log cabins and sod houses got their first books—and in some cases, their only ones—via the circuit riding Methodist preacher and his saddlebags. That is, the Methodists were also a people of the head.

This combination isn't surprising. It was written into the Methodist genetic code from the beginning.

This is not to say that other Christian bodies don't also seek to give a place to both head and heart. But Methodism has traditionally linked the two in what is nothing other than a holy marriage. As in any marriage, the weight of influence lies sometimes to one and then to the other, but always there is something in Methodism that—as Charles Wesley would say—seeks to unite the two so long divided, knowledge and vital piety.

Let me spell it out in rather specific terms. Broadly speaking, Methodism is not usually as academically inclined as the Episcopal or Presbyterian heritages. Neither is it as emotional in worship style as a Pentecostal church or some bodies in the Baptist tradition. In saying this, I am probably offending some persons in each of those bodies, including Methodists. But with predictable exceptions, I think my case holds.

In one sense, as I've already said, it is part of Methodism's genetic code, but it wasn't easy to gain such an insistent balance. A novelist or poet with a psychological bent might argue that the head-heart connection started with Methodism's grandparents, Samuel and Susanna Wesley. Samuel, the never-quite-fulfilled poet, a man of dreams who wouldn't have been trusted with a checkbook if he had had one, was tilted precariously to the heart—and his blood flowed strong in his son Charles, who gave the Methodist movement literally thousands of songs. Susanna, the tough-minded woman who tried to save the Epworth family from poverty by careful management and who valued time and its proper employment as life's greatest trust, gave it a mind—and her clear thinking went into her son John, the master organizer whose skills still have their daily imprint on the Methodist structure.

Of course this is an over-simplification. Samuel Wesley was also a first-rate mind, a scholar whose best dreams were fulfilled in the Oxford achievements of his sons. Nevertheless, he often said to wife Susanna, "I protest, sweetheart, I think our Jack would not attend to the most pressing necessities of nature unless he could give a reason for it!" Thirty-five years after Samuel died, John remembered how his father had often told him, "Child, you think to carry everything by dint of argument. But you will find by and by, how very little is ever done in the world by clear reason." While clear-thinking Susanna was the stabilizing influence in the Wesley marriage, she was also a woman of great heart, a heart that quite surely poured itself in untiring prayer for the souls of her children and in a stubbornness of faith and hope that would not settle for anything less than great believing.

Whatever the competing balances of head and heart in their parentage, as matters were lived out in the lives of John and Charles Wesley, and as a foundation for what would become the Methodist movement, the head had—so to speak—a head start. There was something wonderfully cerebral and esthetically pleasing in the Anglican Church in which the Wesley brothers grew up. To speak the words of the Book of Common Prayer, as John and Charles did day after day, was to train the mind in clarity of thought and precision of language. The orderliness of the Anglican way of life encouraged discipline. There was a religious calendar to guide one's thoughts and daily prayers. If one wanted to chart a path to heaven, here was a good place to begin. John and Charles were achievers; their academic record makes that clear. Where better to turn their energy for achieving than to eternal things? Sheer logic told them that if God and eternity were real, then God and eternity should be the primary human quest.

It was thus that Charles and a few fellow students began the Holy Club at Oxford, the leadership of which John assumed when he returned to Oxford as a Fellow. The Holy Club, with its impressive methodology, was largely a matter of the mind. For one thing, it demanded a commitment of the mind in its regular study of the Scriptures. Its very structure was a logical one. Joining the Holy Club was like entering boot camp with the Marines. All of life was to come under an almost-hourly discipline. Everything about the discipline was logical, thought-through, certain of its purposes and its goals and of the best way to reach those goals. You didn't enter the Holy Club on a wave of emotion but on a reasoned contract. You knew your desired destination, and you were taking to yourself what you perceived, after much thought, to be the surest way to reach that destination. It was primarily an affair of the mind, guided by logical presuppositions. Those zealous Oxford students pursued their goal with the single-mindedness that had blessed their daily scholarship. They were seeking even more than scholarly excellence; they were hoping to find the biblical pearl of great price.

They found much by their discipline but not what they sought. In October, 1735, John and Charles left for America to work in the colony in Georgia. As the brothers embarked on the long journey, they agreed that they "would neither eat meat or drink wine but depend for sustenance on rice and biscuits."[1] Early in December, they concluded that their bodies didn't need as much as they were eating, so they gave up their suppers and "hitherto found no inconvenience."[2] As for a disciplined method, they arose each morning at 4:00, had private prayer until 5:00, then reading the Scriptures until 7:00, when they had breakfast. At 8:00, public prayers with "usually between thirty and forty of our eighty passengers," then from 9:00 to 12:00 John studied German, while Charles wrote sermons.

It was on this voyage, however, that the heart began to lay its claims on John. Among the passengers was a small group of Moravians, a German pietistic body that cared most about the fervor and warmth of religious experience. Several times during the many weeks on the Atlantic, their ship encountered storms that caused John to fear for his life. On January 25, 1736, waves "split the mainsail in pieces, covered the ship, and poured in between the decks."[3] Most of the passengers broke into screams of fear, but the Moravians simply kept on singing, clearly unperturbed. When John inquired of their feelings, they answered that they were not afraid to die. Wesley wrote in his diary, "This was the most glorious day which I have ever hitherto seen." He realized that these German Christians had a personal faith much beyond his own. Without a doubt, both John and Charles knew more Christology and more scripture, but the Moravians had more practicing faith.

On February 6, 1736, the ship landed in Georgia, and the Wesley brothers set out upon their ministry in the new world. It was not a happy experience, and by almost every measure, neither was it a successful one. Charles left several months before John, returning to England by way of Massachusetts. John's experience became more complicated by his romance with Sophia Hopkey, a pretty eighteen-year-old, a romance that never quite materialized and that John handled badly in almost every way.

It is fair to say that John and Charles were happy to escape Georgia and that the people were not sorry to see them go. John was a scholar, preaching to people who must have found it hard to follow his careful reasoning. He devoted most of what one might call his pastoral time to classes in French for a young man, Delamotte, and Sophia Hopkey. As someone has said, his preaching was "too academic for brute man and brute nature."[4]

But there were those Moravians who, as Elsie Harrison said, "came to religion by way of the heart."[5] Their hymns were so often love songs to their Lord, with a mood that later appeared in some of the hymns of Charles Wesley. Peter Bohler was sure he knew what was wrong with John and Charles Wesley. He wrote to Count Zinzendorf, leader of the Moravians, "Of faith in Jesus, they have no other idea than the generality of people have. They justify themselves, therefore they always take it for granted that they believe already and would prove their faith by their works, and thus so plague and torment themselves that they are at heart very miserable."[6] *At heart:* that's where their problem lay. John and Charles were Masters in theology by both accomplishment and title; they knew the Scriptures with understanding in Hebrew and Greek; and they were sure of the truth. But somehow their religion had settled so firmly in their well-trained heads that it couldn't find the way to their hearts.

Then came a wonderful week in May 1738. It began inauspiciously for Charles. He was physically ill; one has the feeling, in reading his story, that he was ill rather frequently at this point in his life, and one wonders how much of it was psychosomatic or to what degree he was simply physically and emotionally exhausted. No matter; in the midst of his illness, a serving woman of modest learning but of great faith—and perhaps a bit of audacity—told Charles that he would not arise from his sickbed until he believed. Much to his credit, Charles didn't brush aside her counsel; instead, he asked question to learn more of her faith.

Two days later, on Sunday, May 21, Charles and John and some friends sang a hymn together, and Charles prayed earnestly and at length. Then he heard a voice: "In the name of Jesus of Nazareth, arise, and believe, and thou shalt be healed of all thy infirmities." Mrs. Turner confessed that she had spoken the words but that she had done so by order of Christ. Charles felt what he called "a strange palpitation of heart," and though he feared to say it, he declared, "I believe, I believe!" One of our finest Wesley scholars, Kenneth Collins, says of the experience, "Charles now understood the graciousness and power of the gospel not simply intellectually, but also in terms of his tempers and affections. His heart as well as his mind now belonged to the Savior."[7] On Tuesday, Charles started to write a poem about his experience. He had done some things with poetry before, following his father's love for this venue, but now he had a particular impulse to write. On the day of his conversion, he had gotten a special sense of the scripture, "I will put a new song into thy mouth," and this poem seemed to fulfill that sense. As he wrote, however, he began also to feel that he should stop because he feared that to write would only lead to pride. A good, godly layman convinced him otherwise, and Wesley finished the poem: "Where shall my wondering soul begin? / How shall I all to heaven aspire?" Who could have imagined that Charles was embarking on a lifetime of hymnody that would produce some seven thousand hymns in the years following?

John, meanwhile, was still struggling. Early in the morning of Wednesday, May 24, during his scripture meditation, he came upon a verse in 2 Peter that moved him deeply: "Whereby are given unto us exceeding great and precious promises: that by these ye might be partakers of the divine nature" (2 Peter 1:4, KJV). That afternoon, while attending evensong at St. Paul's in London, he engaged himself profoundly in the choir's singing of Purcell's anthem, "Out of the deep have I called unto thee, O Lord." Nevertheless, he had no desire to go to a meeting that evening on Aldersgate Street, and he confides in his journal that he went very unwillingly—but moved nevertheless by the fact that when he opened his Bible it was at the passage, "Thou art not far from the kingdom of God."[8]

What happened that evening is best told in John Wesley's own memorable words: "In the evening I went very unwillingly to a society in Aldersgate Street, where one was reading Luther's Preface to the Epistle to the Romans. About a quarter before nine, while he was describing the change which God works in the heart through faith in Christ, I felt my heart strangely warmed. I felt I did trust in Christ, Christ alone for salvation, and an assurance was given me that he had taken away *my* sins, even *mine*, and saved *me* from the law of sin and death" (italics in the original).

There was no persuasive preacher, no emotional music. The Scriptures that had impressed themselves upon him earlier in the day and the theology he heard that night from Luther's commentary were not new to him. But now they were his own possession. He had received them by way of the "heart strangely warmed." His religion had moved from head to heart. This did not negate or minimize the head; rather, it affirmed it. By experience, John now knew that the gospel was for the whole person. What he had studied for so long and had accepted intellectually was now part of his emotive being as well.

Let Charles pick up the story here. "Towards ten, my brother was brought in triumph by a troop of our friends, and declared, 'I believe.' We sang the hymn with great joy and parted with prayer." The hymn they sang was more than likely the one Charles had written the previous day. Now there were two "wondering souls" who knew they were "redeemed from death and sin," two who "should know; should feel my sins forgiven, / Blest with this antepast of heaven."[9]

Not quite three weeks later, John had the opportunity to take his new faith to a place of the head, as he stepped into the pulpit of the revered St. Mary's Church, Oxford. His text was Ephesians 2:8: "For by grace you have been saved through faith." In the sermon, he raised the question, "What faith is it through which we are saved?' and answered that it was "faith in Christ—Christ, and God through Christ." He felt that this faith he now possessed was a faith that was qualitatively different from what he had known before. It was not a matter of his having more faith but of having a very different kind of faith. Experience, the "warmed heart," was surely a crucial element.

This was not the end of the head-heart balancing act. John would struggle again as he followed George Whitefield's encouragement to engage in field preaching and still more when the warmed hearts in some of his converts convinced them that they should preach. The dramatic emotional displays that sometimes came to some of his hearers during his field preaching must surely have unnerved this very rational man. Even Charles was a burden to him at times, when Charles's hymns seemed unduly emotional.

At its best, Methodism has ever since been this congenial relationship between head and heart. Among Christian bodies in the past and in this present day, there are denominations that lean toward the intellectual and others that lean just as surely to the emotional. Methodism, when true to its calling and its heritage, holds them together, uniting the two so long divided, knowledge and vital piety. Methodism would say, "What God has joined together, let no doctrine or movement put asunder."

Chapter 5

WHAT METHODISTS BELIEVE

Methodism has critics (and also some adherents) who believe that a chapter on Methodist beliefs will necessarily be a short chapter. In practice, I may have enabled such thinking. During my years as a pastor, I sometimes met with people who said, "I don't really know what I believe," in which case I would answer cheerfully, "In that case, you're already a Methodist and don't know it." I was trying to be cordial and welcoming, and I certainly didn't mean to put down Methodism, which I love deeply. But in my comment, I added to the feeling that doctrine is incidental to Methodism.

Let me add that, even after forty-five years, I remember with irritation a seminar in a major university (I won't mention the university, and fortunately, I can't recall the name of the professor) when the professor said archly that Methodists don't really have any theology. As the only Methodist in the circle, I knew that I was outnumbered, and I realized as well that I was at an intellectual disadvantage with the professor and several of the students who laughed appreciatively. But the comment stung and is with me still.

In the intervening years, I have come to know that Methodism has a robust theology and that we also have some able theologians. Further, I've come to see that, in its own way, it's a compliment that some people think Methodists don't have a theology and that doctrine doesn't matter to us. It's incorrect, but there's a good reason—with emphasis on *good*—why people think our theology and our doctrine are weak. I'll come to that later. But first, let me tell you, in fairly succinct form, what Methodists believe.

It was John Wesley, the primary founder of Methodism, who first gave the impression that carefully enunciated doctrinal statements aren't too important. As the early Methodist movement swept through England, he prepared a pamphlet describing, as he put it, "the principles and the practice whereby those who are called Methodists are distinguished from other men." Let me pause to note that the term "principles and practice" is an early indication of the Methodist genetic code.

Wesley begins, "The distinguishing marks of a Methodist are not his opinions of any sort." This sounds as if doctrine is no issue whatsoever. He is still more emphatic when he continues, "Whoever, therefore, imagines that a Methodist is a person of such or such an opinion, is grossly ignorant of the whole affair; he mistakes the truth totally."

He then proceeds, however, to offer several "opinions" which he considers fundamental. "We believe that 'all Scripture is given by inspiration of God.'" "We believe the written word of God to be the only and sufficient rule of Christian faith and practice." "We believe Christ to be the eternal, supreme God." To each of those statements Wesley adds a sentence identifying those theological bodies or belief systems whose teachings are different from each of these positions. Then he adds, "BUT as to all opinions which do not strike at the root of Christianity, we think and let think."[1]

This opening declaration seems very broad, but it is also sharply demanding. The very fact that it is, in some ways, so broad makes all the more important those issues on which it is emphatic. The first two are essentially one: the authority of Scripture. In saying that all Scripture is given by inspiration of God, and that the written word of God is the "only and sufficient rule of Christian faith and practice," Wesley is not only drawing a line in the sand but also establishing an acid test for all further discussion. The Scriptures are Methodism's constitution—except that this is a constitution that cannot be amended. Raise any doctrinal issue, ask any ethical question, and Wesley's answer is, What does the Scripture say?

This doesn't mean an end to discussion, but it does tell us the boundaries of the playing field. We may introduce all sorts of data into our discussion: the teachings of various theologians, philosophers and logicians, the insights of psychology and of the physical sciences, and nuances of language. But Scripture is the settled point, and as Methodists—if we take John Wesley seriously—our arguments are with how we understand our authority, not what the authority is. And if we take "authority" seriously, we need to humble ourselves before the authority and ask first what it teaches, not how we can make it accommodate itself to our prejudices or presuppositions.

The second inviolable issue for Wesley is the person and nature of Jesus Christ. If Methodism is indeed a *Christian* religion, then we had better be clear about who we perceive Jesus Christ to be. Wesley leaves no wiggle room: He is the "eternal, supreme God."[2] No other definition is sufficient. If we are content to identify Christ as a landmark teacher, an incomparable example, the most winsome of personalities and the ultimate hero of human history, then we have said lovely and poetic things but things that are, in fact, devastatingly trivial.

When the Methodist movement crossed the Atlantic and shortly found itself in a new nation, and thus free of British rule, Wesley recognized that it was also free of the state church, the Church of England; thus the break from the Anglican Church that he and Charles never made, John saw as a natural act for American Methodism.

He wasn't about to send it on its way without doctrinal moorings, however. He didn't have to search to find a satisfactory document. Wesley had no argument with the basic doctrines of the Church of England and its Thirty-Nine Articles of Religion. The original Methodists in England knew no other doctrinal statement because their official membership was in the Anglican Church. Now, as the Methodist movement was about to become a separate body in America, Wesley provided them with a somewhat condensed version, choosing twenty-four of the thirty-nine. Those that Wesley removed were mostly matters that had more specifically to do with England or that Wesley found redundant and unnecessary. He also did what he loved to do: found fewer words, when he could, to convey the same truth. Wesley was generally sure that people in general and perhaps religious writers in particular used more words than was absolutely necessary. When the founding meeting of American Methodism met in Lovely Lane Chapel, Baltimore, Maryland, from December 24, 1784 to January 2, 1785, the leaders presented Wesley's twenty-four articles as their standard. The Conference added one, "Of the Rulers of the United States of America," declaring their loyalty to the new nation.

The Twenty-Five Articles were not a formal creed, or even a prerequisite for church membership, but "belief in them was a prerequisite qualification for the ministry."[3] As Henry Wheeler wrote at the turn of the twentieth century,

"The Articles of Religion and our Ritual are two important links in the chain that binds the Methodist Episcopal Church to the great historic Church of past ages."[4] Methodism has never sought to separate itself from its grand heritage. Its basic doctrinal statement affirms this bond.

So this is who we Methodists are doctrinally. We have a heritage in the Church of England, and before that in the Catholic Church and in the apostolic church of the first centuries, with its councils and its creeds. We have an open door: as John Wesley said it repeatedly, open to all who wish to flee from the wrath to come. We have an open heart, one that cares about every human soul regardless of ethnic or racial heritage or level of culture or learning. We have an open mind with the boundaries of the heritage that has been given to us in Christ and his body, the church.

What then did John Wesley mean when he declared that "the distinguishing marks of a Methodist are not his opinions of any sort"?[5] Just this, that John Wesley is one of the most pragmatic of persons and that he hoped to bring together a pragmatic—and therefore, highly practical—body of believers. If you're looking for a Bible verse that summarizes John Wesley's feelings about a true Methodist, it seems to me that you'll find it in our Lord's Sermon on the Mount: "you will know them by their fruit" (Matthew 7:20, CEB). Wesley was sure that, in the end, nothing was as important as the way Christians in general and Methodists in particular lived out their faith.

It's no wonder, then, that when Wesley describes the true Methodist, he spends some ninety percent of his description discussing conduct rather than doctrine. Mind you, neither is it surprising that he puts the descriptions of this ideal believer in biblical language and weaves doctrinal allusions throughout the whole. Having declared the preeminence of the Bible and making clear that Methodists hold to the classical doctrines of Christianity, he describes how we live out this faith—and Scripture and doctrine give it form and substance.

Wesley is at his happy—indeed, rollicking—best as he describes what Methodists look like. If you had interrupted him at intervals to advise him that you knew Methodists who weren't as wonderful as his description, I sense that he would have answered with the back of his hand and a smile, "Just wait a while. They'll get there. Because this is who we are."

A Methodist is one, its founder says, "who has the love of God in his heart." "God is the joy of his heart, the desire of his soul."[6] As a result, this person "is therefore happy in God, yea, always happy." This is not because he or she is oblivious to what is happening. Rather, it is because of a careful study of all the facts. Specifically, "having found redemption through [Christ's] blood, and forgiveness of his sins, he cannot but rejoice whenever he looks back on the horrible pit out of which he has been delivered; when he sees all his transgressions blotted out and all his iniquities. He cannot but rejoice whenever he looks on the state wherein he now is, 'being justified freely and having peace with God through our Lord Jesus Christ.' "[7]

All of us know that we shape so much of life by our attitudes. Wesley knew this, too, and preached it fervently. His Methodist is someone who "gives thanks in everything," whether full or empty, "in ease or pain, whether in sickness or health, whether in life or death, confident that "only good can come from the Father." Thus Methodists don't worry; instead they pray—"his heart is ever lifted up to God at all times and in all places." "In retirement [that is, privacy] or company, in leisure, business, or conversation, his heart is ever with the Lord. . . . he walks with God continually." As a result of such a thought life this person "loves his neighbour as himself; he loves every person as his own soul."[8]

Because the one desire of such a person is purity of life and heart, "none can take from him what he desires, seeing that he loves not the world nor any of the things of the world."[9] After all, if our greatest treasure is purity and goodness, who can take it from us unless by our consent?

A Methodist's "one business" is "to advance the glory of God." This is true whether he or she is at home or walking by the way, whether lying down or rising up. Whether dressing for the day, working, eating, or drinking, Methodists have "one invariable rule: 'Whatsoever ye do, in word or deed, do it all in the name of the Lord Jesus, giving thanks to God and the Father by him.'"[10]

This is heady language, and one's first inclination is to say that Wesley doesn't know the kind of world in which we live. It's clear that Wesley sensed that people would raise such an objection and continued, "Nor do the customs of the world hinder his running the race that is set before him. He knows that vice does not lose its nature, though it becomes ever so fashionable."[11] Wesley could well have written that phrase, "though it becomes ever so fashionable" for our time and place, a culture that lives by public opinion polls and popularity charts and seeks thus to shape us into its mold.

Although Wesley wrote his analysis of the culture roughly two and a half centuries ago, for a nation just moving from the agricultural to the industrial age, one senses that the difference is a matter of degrees not of inclinations. He warns his people—using biblical quotations—that they should not "fare sumptuously every day," a matter that in our day finds a fascinating expression in television's food channels and in daily conversations about places to eat (including, ironically, the best prospects among fast food stops). So, too, we should not "adorn ourselves with gold or costly apparel"[12]—in our culture, the entertainment personality who gushes about her more than a hundred pairs of shoes, or the athlete who gets a prince's reward for endorsing a gym shoe.

Wesley climaxes with what was for him the most important issue of all (and again, on his basis in the Scriptures): this person "does good unto all men," whether neighbours or strangers, friends or enemies. And this goodness extends through all territory of life, "in every possible kind; not only to their bodies by 'feeding the hungry, clothing the naked, visiting those that are sick or in prison;' but much more does he labor to do good to their souls."[13]

"THESE," Wesley says, "are the principles and practices of our sect: THESE are the marks of a true Methodist. By these alone do those who are so called desire to be distinguished from other men." As Wesley reaches the conclusion of his little pamphlet, he recognizes how any thoughtful reader is likely to respond to what he has written. Some are likely to say, "Why, these are only the common, fundamental principles of Christianity!" Wesley answers, quite gleefully, "That is what I mean. It is the truth. There are no other fundamental principles. I wish to God that all men knew that I, and all who follow my judgment (that is, Methodists), do vehemently refuse to be distinguished from other men, by any but the common principles of Christianity—the plain, old Christianity that I teach, renouncing and detesting all other marks of distinction."[14]

That is, a true Methodist "thinks, speaks, and lives according to the method laid down in the revelation of Jesus Christ." Therefore, "from real Christians, of whatever denomination they be, we earnestly desire not to be distinguished at all"[15] (this, I remind you, from the *Anglican* priest who came to transforming faith while hearing a *Lutheran* paper read at a *Moravian* meeting).

Wesley then writes sentences by which many know him. They are powerful sentences, as fine as any in Christian literature, but they are rightly understood only in the context of

Wesley's full document. "Is thy heart right, as my heart is with thine? I ask no farther question. If it be, give me thy hand. For opinions, or terms, let us not destroy the work of God. Dost thou love and serve God? It is enough. I give thee the right hand of fellowship."[16]

Probably the reason Methodists seem so often to know little of what they believe is because our "distinguishing marks" are in the way we—historically—have aimed to live rather than by particular doctrines. Let me say it this way. If one asks a Baptist what he or she believes, the Baptist is likely to point to believer baptism, by immersion. If you ask, "But don't you believe in the Trinity, and that Jesus Christ is the Son of God," this Baptist is likely to reply, "Of course. But that isn't what makes us different." So, too, with a Seventh Day Adventist, or a Pentecostal or a devout Catholic: ask for his or her belief and he lists what is distinctive about his or her church body.

Wesley disclaimed any such unique beliefs. He insisted on the basic, traditional teachings of the church, delivered through the Scriptures, and that those teachings be lived out in the most practical, joyful, and effective fashion. Even those matters that the Methodists emphasized—religious experience, personal accountability, and personal and social holiness—were a means to an end, and the end was truly godly living: the kind of living that is salt and light in a decaying and dark world.

It's wonderfully simple and magnificently complex. It is within the reach of any believer because it is the salvation for which our Lord died. But it isn't for religious dilettantes, on the one hand, or for religious hair-splitters, on the other. And it isn't easy. Whoever said that it should be? Not Jesus. He said we'd have to take up our cross if we would follow him.

What a wonderful way to live! Have you ever thought of being a Methodist?

Chapter 6

A PEOPLE MOVING TO PERFECTION

Perfect is one of those words that we use both to bless and to discredit. When we've tried hard and someone says, "That was perfect!" we're elated. It can be as big as a medical procedure or as transient as a pot roast, but "perfect" is the ultimate praise. On the other hand, you know that a discussion is on hazardous ground when someone says, "You think you're so *perfect*!" When a friend says, "You're a perfectionist, aren't you," there's usually a tone of sympathy as they say it. Indeed, you may have used that term to describe yourself, knowing that it was partly an invitation for respect and partly a plea for mercy.

Nevertheless, all of us hope for perfection in matters that count most. No one wants a surgeon who's satisfied to fail once in a while; we want him or her to aim for perfection, especially when we're the one under care. Nor can we imagine an airline advertising, "Our pilots have a high degree of success." We prefer perfection!

Still, in the day-by-day business of living, most of us are quick to say, "Nobody's perfect." At the same time, however, we feel we're copping out when we argue, "There's no use trying to be perfect," because common sense reminds us that we certainly don't aim to be imperfect. Imperfection, after all, is no achievement.

There's no place where perfection should be more at home than in religion, and there's no place where it is more elusive. The Pharisees of Jesus' time may have been the greatest perfection-seekers of all time. And what did it get them? With all their Herculean efforts, they gave us an adjective and won a place in our dictionaries: "Pharisaic: practicing or advocating strict observation of external terms and ceremonies of religion or conduct without regard to spirit; self-righteous; sanctimonious."[1]

It's the external/spirit split that makes perfection in matters of religion so difficult. Perfection in medicine, sports, or accounting is pretty much a matter of external, measurable factors, but perfection in religion has more to do with the spirit—and who can define matters of the spirit? How, that is, except by things external? This is the sort of issue the apostle James had in mind when he told off some self-righteous folks. "Imagine a brother or sister who is naked and never has enough food to eat. What if one of you said, 'Go in peace! Stay warm! Have a nice meal!'? What good is it if you don't actually give them what their body needs?" (James 2:15-16, CEB).

Let me complicate the scene still further. Suppose you have the right spirit within, and do the practical, helpful thing—then, as you walk away, think smugly to yourself, "What a wonderful person am I!" And just like that, you've become self-righteous, discrediting the work you've just done.

It's enough to make us average souls decide simply to do the best we can and not worry about becoming saints and perhaps, in the process, to become rather smug in our mediocrity. Unfortunately, Jesus won't let us off that easily. He set the bar ultimately high: "Be perfect, therefore, as your heavenly Father is perfect" (Matthew 5:48, NIV). John and Charles Wesley couldn't get away from that kind of command. As a result, they insisted on going on to perfection.

The pursuit of perfection is neither an easy life to live nor an easy gospel to preach. Wesley and his best adherents would have had an easier time of it if they had laid aside or minimized the call to perfection. But if they had done so, they wouldn't have been Methodists—and neither would there have been any reason for their coming into existence. Christianity didn't need another infusion of halfway-disciples; such have always been a glut on the religious market. Christianity needed a people who were strikingly different, a people so persuaded of Christ and so earnest in their desire to be like him that no other goal would satisfy. John Wesley was convinced that this message was Methodism's "grand depositum," its very reason for existence.

John Wesley used several terms interchangeably: perfection, holiness, sanctification, and perfect love. Because we use the terms interchangeably, it's proper to call them synonyms. But they are also complementary. Each word and each concept adds to our understanding of the others and helps to make up the whole of what we mean is a profoundly Christian life.

Let me interrupt myself at this point on something which may seem peripheral but which is probably the proverbial "elephant in the room" and which, until we discuss it, is likely to distract from everything else. I am referring to the discomfort many feel when we mention the words *holy* and *holiness*. Something about these words seems other-worldly and quite out of reach for the majority of us.

Wesley didn't see it that way, and neither should we. He was sure that we humans "are made to be happy in God." He urged parents to remind their children early and often, "[God] made you, and he made you to be happy in him, and nothing else can make you happy." United with this belief was Wesley's deep and frequently expressed conviction that we cannot be happy without being holy. "I am convinced true religion or holiness cannot be without cheerfulness . . .

and that true religion has nothing sour, austere, unsociable in it." And then, one of Wesley's iconic quotes is: "Sour godliness is the devil's religion."[2]

One of British Methodism's finest preachers in the twentieth century, William E. Sangster, contrasted Christian holiness with Stoics, Pharisees, ascetic monks, and Puritans, who are, he said, "for the most part, hard and cheerless souls. They seem to have been quarried, not born. Noble and austerely splendid as their best types unquestionably are, they fail in one of the chief tests of true sanctity; and prove that this is a false path for us. They are not *happy*, and the flaw is fatal" (italics in original). Sangster reminds us that joy is "a necessary mark of the saint."[3]

This belief in happiness as inseparable from holiness when we remember that the Methodist definition of holiness was *perfect love*. What is this "perfect love"? It is

> A rest where all our soul's desire
> Is fixed on things above;
> Where doubt, and pain, and fear expire,
> Cast out by perfect love.[4]

So what is implied in being a "perfect Christian"? Wesley answers, "The loving God with all our heart, and mind, and soul" (Deuteronomy 6:5, paraphrased).

For Methodism, there is no such thing as love of God unless it shows itself also in our love of one another. Because God is "invisible to our eyes," Wesley writes, "we are to serve Him in our neighbour." God receives this action,

Wesley explains, as if we had done it to God in person, "standing visibly before us." Wesley was more than emphatic about this. He insisted that any religion or piety that is not centered on the active love of God and neighbor is a false religion. As Professor Irv Brendlinger has put it, "the practical result of loving God included love for one's neighbour. One could not serve or love God in a vacuum."[5]

Wesley always acknowledged that even the most earnest Christians may err by reason of their ignorance and mistakes. "Indeed, I do not expect to be freed from actual mistakes till this mortal puts on immortality. I believe this to be a natural consequence of the soul's dwelling in flesh and blood. For we cannot now *think* at all, but by the mediation of those bodily organs, which have suffered equally with the rest of our frame. And hence we cannot avoid sometimes *thinking wrong*, till this corruptible shall have put on incorruption" (italics in original).[6] The issue was that in all things—in our deeds, surely, but just as certainly in our words and thoughts, we should act out of love for God and love for our fellow creatures.

Without a doubt, those who approach life with such a conviction and such a faith live happier lives—and make others happier in the process; not by preaching to them but by caring about them. This includes those who live with us day and night, work with us, study with us, engage us at the daily routines of commerce, and with whom we communicate by face-to-face conversation, by telephone, by written letter, and by e-mail and all of the extensions of e-mail.

This is a high goal, indeed. John Wesley admitted as much. "If we are fools," he wrote, in confessing such a way of life, "yet as fools bear with us." "We do expect to love God with all our heart, and our neighbour as ourselves."[7]

What is the manner by which perfection comes to a believer? Wesley answers, "I believe this perfection is always wrought in the soul by a simple act of faith; consequently in an instant. But I believe in a gradual work both preceding and following that instant." And when will it happen? Wesley continues, "I believe this instant generally is the instant of death, the moment before the soul leaves the body. But I believe it may be ten, twenty, or forty years before."[8]

Wesley believed that we all must be perfect in order to enter heaven because there can be no imperfection there, so at the least or the most, one will be made perfect by God's grace at the instant of death—but it can happen at any point in the Christian life. Such perfection is certainly not for the faint of heart. The early Methodist hymn books were set up in sections titled for the various experiences and periods of the Christian life, and there was a large section under the classification, "For Believers Fighting, Watching, Praying," and another for "Persons Convinced of Backsliding." One of the loveliest lines in the latter group of hymns seeks help from Jesus, who is "More full of grace than I of sin." It might be a struggle; indeed, it almost surely would be. But God in love was on their side, wanting holiness for them more even than the most devout would want it for themselves.

There has been some controversy among various Methodist theologians and different Methodist bodies as to the significance of a particular, identifiable experience, often referred to as "a second definite work of grace." Some of the loveliest Christians I have known have been persons who testified to such an experience, but I have known others who were equally admirable who identified no such event. Grateful as I am for a variety of faith experiences, beginning with the night of my conversion, I am uneasy with a theology that ties itself too closely to experience. Experiences are as fallible as the people who experience them; thus an experience may seem to lose its validity when the person passes through times of emotional stress. I rest more upon the witness of Scripture. I worry, too, about the complacency that sometimes comes with a religious experience: the feeling, "Now I've got it made." Wesley insisted that "a believer daily grows in grace, comes nearer and nearer to perfection," and that "we ought to be continually pressing after it, and to exhort all others so to do."[9]

Whatever one's particular theology about sanctification or Christian perfection, one matter should be undeniable: to be a believer is to be a growing soul. The analogy offered by the new birth says as much: a person is born with the expectation of growing. The apostle noted that all the ministries in the church—apostles, prophets, evangelists, pastors, teachers—existed so that believers might grow. Those who feel that they have experienced a special event in holiness should be, of all people, those most passionate about growing. Who, after all, would be more convinced of the worth of a consistent walk with Christ than those who have known a special marker in their journey?

How, then, does such growth happen? And how might one come to the holiness of perfect love? The Methodists had the secret in their name itself and in the way of life that led to their name. They had a *method*, and the method was born in the Holy Club at Oxford, years before either Charles or John had experienced the warm heart that characterized their work and the emerging Methodist movement. The rules of the Holy Club were geared to an academic life, for persons more able to control the use of their time and not the kind of rules that a collier, a factory worker, a farm hand, or an eighteenth-century mother could fulfill.

Nevertheless, the Holy Club idea demonstrated the importance of discipline; not only self-discipline but also the discipline that comes from belonging to a group of persons who have also chosen to live a disciplined life. Over the centuries, the secret remains the same. Occasionally, someone gains passing attention with a particular technique but, in the end, the way to consistent Christian living and to true holiness remains the same: prayer, study of the Scriptures and other religious materials, giving of one's time and resources, instruction in the faith, both private and public worship, celebration of the sacrament, and serving others. It's really quite simple—which, in turn, is why it's so difficult.

The major reason all of this is so difficult is not the practices themselves. Some are demanding and perhaps tedious, and they take time. But they're manageable. The problem is in the hidden element. It isn't enough that we do all these things; it is absolutely crucial that we do them in the right spirit. If we pray, give, work, and study in order to advance ourselves and to be blessed, then we'll miss the mark. The secret is to do these things to please and glorify God and to bless others. I'm quite sure that some people move from being mean secular people to being mean religious people— and I think I prefer the former to the latter because the latter become ensconced in their own righteousness.

After all, if it's our own benefit that drives us, then our motivation is still self-centered. True, others benefit in some measure, but the motivation or goal is still the self. This focus reminds us again that true holiness is *pure love*: love of God and love of others. This result can happen only if there is a true conversion of the heart and life. I would add, from my own years of seeking such a life and urging others in the pursuit, it calls for a *continuing* conversion. Every day you and I encounter people, conversations, influences, so every day we need new commitment to a godly life and renewed love for God and others.

Methodism's early emphasis on small groups—accountability groups—was a big motivating factor. There were plenty of dangers, of course, because all groups are made up of human beings, and human judgment is fallible. At least there was the possibility of a correcting, loving voice.

Also, there was Methodism's teaching that holiness must be both personal and social. Believers knew that they must watch over their own souls, but they also knew that the road to heaven is not a solitary one; they must care for their fellow travelers, no matter what the traveler's need or person.

The goal was to go on to perfection. In the words of the apostle Paul, "God's goal is for us to become mature adults— to be fully grown, measured by the standard of the fullness of Christ" (Ephesians 4:13, CEB). With Paul we might well confess, "It's not that I have already reached this goal or have already been perfected, but I pursue it, so that I may grab hold of it because Christ grabbed hold of me for just this purpose" (Philippians 3:12, CEB).

And that's it. This is the purpose for which Christ "grabbed hold" of you and me. That being so, how dare we be satisfied to stop short of it? Who wants to stop short—that is, to be imperfect—when Christ's goal for us is perfection?

Chapter 7

THE REDEEMED PERSON IN
AN UNREDEEMED SOCIETY

Methodism came to birth in a stratified society, one in which both the advantaged and the disadvantaged considered that this was the way life was supposed to be. Some people inherited privilege, and some inherited poverty; both had made peace with the system. It was also a time of epochal change as England moved headlong into the industrial revolution. This change promised to add new strain to the social and economic structure. Expanding industry would give some clever and creative individuals a chance to rise out of their poverty, but for each such instance, many others would fall into a more debasing kind of poverty. The move from a rural culture to that of industrial cities would add further dimensions to the dehumanizing process.

Somehow the Methodist movement understood from the beginning that it is not enough to save individual souls; the gospel insists that we seek also to redeem society. They understood that if one follows the Christ who condemned the rich man for ignoring the needs of poor, sick, hungry Lazarus on his doorstep, then one needs to do something about one's own generation of the poor, sick, and hungry.

I say "somehow" because the Wesley brothers were hardly the sort one would choose to begin a social and economic revolution. True, the family in the Epworth rectory was not rich, but if Samuel had been a better manager, neither would they have been poor. By nature and heritage, John and Charles were bred to be middle class. They grew up in a highly literate home with a taste for the finer things. Their years at Oxford lifted that taste still higher. In truth, their experiences in Epworth village might easily have made them thoroughgoing snobs. They had good reason to resent the rough villagers who burned their father's crops and set fire more than once to the rectory. If they had decided that the poor were poor simply because they were mean, drunken, and shiftless, an objective observer would have understood. Besides, every village rector knew that his security lay with the squire not with the rabid poor.

It was popular in Wesley's day, as it is with some today, to say that the poor "are poor only because they are idle."

Wesley called this idea "wickedly, devilishly false." Rather, Wesley said, "I love the poor. In many of them I find pure genuine grace, unmixed with paint, folly, and affectation. ... The poor are the Christians."[1] Where did John Wesley get such an outlook? Partly, for sure, from Susanna, primary teacher to the Wesley brood. She taught her children to treat their servants with respect, never addressing them by their first name without adding a title. I suspect that it was an extension of this training that caused John, in his adult life, to remove his hat in respect when a street beggar thanked him for a coin. We see Susanna's regard for individuals, regardless of their rank, when early in the Methodist movement young Thomas Maxfield—unordained and from an Anglican point of view, not properly educated—began to preach. John was properly upset, but his mother said, "But take care what you do with respect to that young man, for he is as surely called of God to preach as you are."[2] For a culture in which the standards were set by the state church and the established clergy enjoyed being established, this statement was a dramatic declaration of human equality. It reflected the spirit that infused all of Susanna's teaching and influence on her children.

As I see it, an equally important factor in the Methodist concern for the least and most unattractive of humans came from Methodism's theology—that all persons are sinners and that Christ died for all. As I have noted elsewhere, Charles's hymns spoke of Christ's death for harlots, thieves, and the worst of criminals and added that he himself belonged to that number. It may be a cliché, but it is true that the ground is level around the cross. If Christ died equally for all persons, then all are in equal need and deserve the best of our embracing care. This is true even though the need expresses itself in different ways, so some seem more base and some more appealing than others. God's love is not discriminating nor should ours be.

So Methodism became not only the body of spiritual awakening in much of the British Isles, but it became also the key player in an astonishing era of social and economic reform. Some historians have said that if it had not been for the Methodist revival, England would have had as bloody a revolution as France. Again and again, Wesley reminded whomever would hear that the Methodist movement had come into existence, "Not to form any new sect; but to reform the nation, particularly the Church, and to spread scriptural holiness over the land." It is significant that he saw their calling not to reform the Church, but "the nation, particularly the Church," and that he saw this happening not by political action but by the spread of "scriptural holiness over the land."[3] Clearly, he expected that if spiritual renewal came to the nation, then its influence would be felt at every level. In Wesley's mind, "scriptural holiness" was also social holiness. "Christianity," he said in one of his discourses on the Sermon on the Mount, "is essentially a social religion, and to turn it into a solitary one is to destroy it."[4] He wasn't about to let that happen.

The late Professor Philip Watson noted that when early Methodists met in their class or society gatherings they would sometimes sing, "In Jesu's name, behold, we meet, / Far from an evil world retreat, / And all its frantic ways," which might make one think that Christians were turning their backs on the world. But Watson explained that in the next verse the hymn declared, "Not in the tombs we pine to dwell, / Nor in the dark monastic cell, / By vows and grates confined." Rather, "Freely to all ourselves we give, / Constrained by Jesu's love to live / The servants of mankind."[5] These great souls, coming from simple lives of no obvious importance or influence, believed that they were redeemed so that they might serve all humanity, to make a difference in the world and time in which they lived. They had heard, as expressed in another Wesleyan hymn, "the widow's and the orphan's groan," and now seeking to relieve "the poor and helpless," they were ready "My life, my all, for them to give."[6]

Wesley spelled this out in sermons, tracts, and pamphlets. The publishing arms of Methodism sent out hundreds of thousands of publications to a population that Wesley was encouraging to become readers. These sermons and teaching pamphlets attacked a wide range of social and private evils. Smuggling was common at the time, as a way of avoiding the excise tax. People who were otherwise honorable bought supplies from smugglers to avoid the tax. Wesley preached against such conduct in sermons and in pamphlets. Bribes were common to buy votes in local elections. The Methodists preached against such a perversion of voting and removed from membership any who were guilty of doing so.

John Wesley not only preached and produced pamphlets, but he also wrote for popular secular publications. In a letter for publication in *Lloyd's Evening Post,* which he later enlarged into a pamphlet, Wesley wrote, "I ask first, why are thousands of people starving, perishing for want in every part of England."[7] By his constant travel and his work with the poor, Wesley probably knew the national scene better than anyone. He asked why some "could only afford to eat a little coarse food every other day" in a land where others had "the necessities, the conveniences, the superfluities of life." He wrote that perhaps the remedy "exceeds all the wisdom of man to tell," but he suggested some places to begin. For instance, bring down the price of oats for food by "reducing the number of horses," "by laying an additional tax on gentlemen's carriages," the luxury automobiles of that day. How can a society reduce the price of pork and poultry? "By repressing luxury, either by example, by laws, or both."[8]

Wesley lived the example and urged his people to do the same. Pragmatic as he was, he knew that example wouldn't reach some of the comfortable and hard-hearted, in which case there should be laws, as well. On one occasion, some of the more well-to-do Methodists told Wesley that he didn't know the value of money. He answered in a sermon, "I have heard today that I do not know the value of money. What?

Don't I know that twelve pence make a shilling, and twenty-one shillings a guinea? Don't I know that if given to God, it's worth heaven, through Christ? And don't I know that if hoarded and kept, it's worth damnation to the man who hoards it?"[9] He agreed fully that money itself was not evil, but the way we use it can surely be evil. Wesley feared its enticing power. As he told one of his sisters, "Money never stays with me. It would burn me if it did. I throw it out of my hands as soon as possible, lest it should find its way into my heart."[10]

The Methodists didn't stop with sermons, pamphlets, and books, nor with airy discussions on the root causes of poverty. They worked at it at every level. When Wesley was asked to define "neighbor," he answered, "every man in the world."[11] In everyday contacts, Methodists were taught to be polite, honest, gentle, loving, kind, and courteous to everyone. Wesley knew that learning is the way out of poverty and also one of the finer pleasures of life, and he turned thousands of illiterate English people into reading Methodists. John Telford wrote in the 14th edition of the *Encyclopedia Britannica* that no man in the eighteenth century "did so much to create a taste for good reading and to supply it with books at the lowest prices." Oscar Sherwin puts it succinctly: "Wesley helped to democratize learning."[12] Clearly, Wesley felt that to save souls was also to save minds.

One marvels at all the institutional activity of the early Methodist movement. A bare two years after Aldersgate,

John Wesley took on the responsibility of Kingswood School, which George Whitefield had started earlier. There was a need, and Methodism meant to fill it. So, too, with an orphanage and a home for aged widows.

One of the finest efforts of early Methodism was its concern for the physical health of the common people. It began with appointing persons to serve in visitation to the sick; the person so appointed was to see each sick person in the fellowship three times a week. It was soon obvious that the need was far greater than anticipated. Most of the poor could not afford prescribed medicines. Wesley got the help of an apothecary and a surgeon to treat those with chronic illnesses. They treated both Methodists and non-members equally. Because there was nothing sectarian about illness, there should be nothing sectarian about care and healing.

Wesley's convictions led, not surprisingly, to another publication, *Primitive Physic*. The first edition under that title came out in 1747. It addressed medical problems in simple, straight-forward fashion, arranged in alphabetical order. Revised editions came out regularly and frequently. By the twenty-third edition, there were listings for 288 diseases and disorders, with 824 remedies. It is easy today to smile at some of the counsel, but this does not by any means discredit it. Wesley used the best knowledge available at the time, and as a scholar trained in the sciences, he had a foundation for judgment. He readily corrected himself from one edition to another. The aim was to meet the needs of vast numbers of persons who otherwise would get no medical attention.

Then there was the issue of slavery. In 1774, Wesley published *Thoughts upon Slavery*, basing much of the writing on a Quaker abolitionist, Anthony Benezet. Historians and biographers often note that the last letter John Wesley wrote a few days before his death was to William Wilberforce, urging him to continue his parliamentary fight against what Wesley called "that execrable villainy, which is the scandal of religion, of England, and of human nature." As for slavery in America, Wesley called it "the vilest that ever saw the sun."[13]

His followers did not forget Wesley's opposition to slavery. The most notable, of course, was Wilberforce, the brilliant parliamentary voice of reform. But the message had reached the Methodist masses. When petitioning against slavery reached its peak in 1832–1833—roughly a generation after John Wesley's death—more than 95 percent of all Wesleyan Methodists signed the petitions, making them by far the largest nonconformist voice in England.

The Methodist influence continued in other areas of human need as well. Professor Oscar Sherwin notes that the leaders of the factory acts movement were all influenced by Methodism. John Oastler and Michael Sadler grew up in Methodism and were for a time local preachers. Lord Shaftesbury (Anthony Ashley Cooper, 1801–1885), who worked both in Parliament and outside it to improve the treatment of the insane and the living conditions of England's poor and was popularly known as "Friend of the Poor," confessed that he owed his spiritual life to a Methodist servant.[14]

The Wesley brothers were a people of their time and place in many of their political convictions. They would hardly have understood democracy as we know it today. They believed in government by kings, though John Wesley never hesitated to criticize the moral conduct of the British kings where it was justified, nor was he silent in insisting that they should care for the poor and institute policies that would make for full employment.

John Richard Green, a major English historian of the late nineteenth century, took what might seem to be a sociologist's view of Wesley's influence when he wrote in his *History of the English People*, "The Methodists themselves were the least result of the Methodist revival. . . . A yet nobler result of the religious revival was the steady attempt which has never ceased from that day to this to remedy the guilt, the ignorance, the physical suffering, the social degradation of the profligate and poor."[15] Someone who thinks of Methodism as primarily a soul-saving body might resent Professor Green's statement. Certainly it is true that Wesley insisted that his preachers remember that they had nothing to do but to save souls. Nevertheless, Green's statement is a powerful tribute to the social, political, and moral influence of true religion. I'm quite sure that John Wesley would not agree that "the Methodists themselves were the least result of the Methodist revival,"[16] but perhaps he would be happy to see that his convictions about social holiness had borne the kind of fruit Professor Green described.

As we move later in our study to the story of Methodism in America, we will see a continuing application of Wesley's social passion. Wesley, the preacher on horseback (and in a carriage in the latter years of his life), will be multiplied many fold in the frontier preachers, led by Francis Asbury, who by himself traveled more miles than Wesley. Their influence on the democracy that was coming to birth in America is difficult to measure but unquestionably profound. Following Wesley's example, the Methodists were into the publishing and distribution of reading material almost from the beginning, though the range of their books and their vigor in attacking social evils were not up to Wesley's record.

Nor were the American Methodists as clear a voice on the issue of slavery. They were at the outset, but the economic importance of slavery to the cotton industry of the south made it easy to mute the fight against slavery. In time, the issue divided American Methodism and, as we shall see, split the church into north and south even before the nation itself broke into two parts.

Some of the most forceful and influential voices in the struggle for women's suffrage came from Methodism, and it is not surprising, therefore, that Methodism was among the leaders in the ordaining of women for ministry in the church. Methodism was no doubt the single largest denominational voice in the prohibition movement of the late nineteenth and early twentieth centuries. Though the movement itself was later repudiated in legislation, the lasting impact cannot be denied. Alcohol addiction and abuse in twenty-first-century America is still a major social and economic problem, but it cannot be compared with the problem that existed in eighteenth-century America prior to the rise of the prohibition movement.

Virtually every religious body, Catholic and Protestant, was involved in the battle for racial justice in the 1960s in America. One cannot fairly say that Methodism led the way, but it was a factor all through the ranks. It continues to be a strong voice in an issue that still falls far short of the Kingdom standard.

The Methodist voice, in matters of world peace, is not convincing. Our public declarations are well-meaning and often well-spoken but not widely persuasive. Almost everyone believes in peace, but few speak wisely enough and convincingly enough to make a difference.

In a variety of other social issues, including such vital matters as right to life and abortion, proper medical care for all, poverty, and the distribution of wealth, we are in a spiritual malaise. The problem is partly intellectual: we have become so good at seeing the nuances of every issue that we can no longer find a clear line between right and wrong. Further, the current decline in denominational influence has reduced public religions pronouncements to a place somewhere between the inconsequential and the amusing. One wonders how a twenty-first-century John Wesley would address a time and culture like ours.

One thing is sure. It is no time to pull into our shell and pull the shell in after us. It is a time for profound, prayerful, courageous thought. Because if holiness is true—as indeed it is—one of its expressions will always be *social* holiness. The redeemed soul can never be content for its generation to live in an unredeemed society.

Chapter 8

SINGING LIKE A METHODIST

It was the Scottish patriot, Andrew Fletcher of Saltoun, who said it, and he did so when John Wesley was a year old and before Charles Wesley was born, but it describes perfectly a key secret of Methodism: "If a man were permitted to make all the ballads, he need not care who should make the laws of a nation."[1] The Methodist revival set the British Isles singing, and I submit that those songs did more to change the character and life of England in that century than any of its laws. Sometimes the singing initiated the change of heart and conscience and sometimes reinforced it, but always the singing was there.

This singing then crossed the ocean, and the Methodist circuit riders carried its mood and message to the frontiers of the new land called America. Much of the time the singing was a cappella, not because the vocal quality was so excellent but because much of the time no musical instruments were available. But the words carried the joy, the hope, and the convictions of a redeemed people. It seemed sometimes that they could hardly help themselves; in the language of Fanny Crosby, America's most prolific song writer (who also identified herself as a Methodist), "I sing, for I cannot be silent."[2] When you know something deeply and love what you know, you want to put it into words; and when you want those words to take on life and to become more firmly placed in your memory and to permeate your very being, you want the words to have a tune.

The Methodists didn't invent this idea. People have been singing for as long as any of us can imagine. Perhaps they caught it from the creation song, "while the morning stars sang in unison" (Job 38:7, CEB). Certainly Israel knew all about singing, as demonstrated by the book of Psalms. The first Christians sang in a variety that the apostle Paul called "psalms, hymns, and spiritual songs" (Ephesians 5:19, CEB). The monks and nuns sang their prayers, and Martin Luther set his new congregants to singing songs that he himself wrote. But I dare to say that no one ever did it better than the Methodists, and no movement was ever more thoroughly shaped by its singing than those Methodists.

Charles Wesley was the key figure, of course; he was the house musician for the Methodist revival. In one sense, John got an even earlier start, even before his transforming Aldersgate experience. With my prejudice toward good hymnody, I dare to say that this earlier experience helped prepare John for Aldersgate.

It came by way of the Moravians. Their own remarkable spiritual movement had begun August 13, 1727, and hymns played a part from the outset. On the long and often trying voyage from England to Georgia in 1735–1736, the German Moravians sang; not only during their worship periods but also during the storms that threatened to destroy the ship. They were hymns the Moravians had written in their periods of persecution, and they had a quality quite different from the kind of music John Wesley had previously known. As G. Elsie Harrison put it, they "assaulted [Wesley's] tender heart. They were so wistful, so human and so real. They were almost love songs." And their mood was very different from "the effort and the strain of his own Holy Club."[3]

In Wesley's zeal to build a Christian community in the Georgia colony, he set out to publish a hymn book—the first in America, it seems. Wesley translated several hymns from the German and used a number of the Moravian songs he had come to love. His heart was yet to be "strangely warmed," but the warmth in these Moravian hymns obviously expressed some of his latent longing. Consider:

> With faith I plunge me in this sea,
> Here is my hope, my joy, my rest;
> Hither, when hell assails, I flee,
> I look into my Saviour's breast:

> Away, sad doubt and anxious fear!
> Mercy is all that's written there.[4]

The hymns added vitality to the otherwise stiff ritual. Wesley sang them to himself as he went about his days and often at the bedside of sick parishioners.

Such hymns must have prepared John for the hymn his brother Charles wrote two days after his own spiritual awakening, then led the group in singing the night John and company arrived to testify to John's experience at Aldersgate:

> Where shall my wondering soul begin?
> How shall I all to heaven aspire?
> A slave redeemed from death and sin,
>   A brand plucked from eternal fire,
> How shall I equal triumphs raise
> Or sound my great Deliverer's praise?[5]

This was stuff of the overflowing heart, and as is the case with the fullest conversion, the heart becomes broad in its love for others. So the proper son of the Epworth parsonage, the earnest Oxford scholar, called out to "Harlots, and publicans, and thieves! / He spreads His arms to embrace you all." And perhaps with a memory of the pharisaic quality that sometimes had tainted the Holy Club: "No need of him the righteous have; / He came the lost to seek and save."[6]

As the Methodists began to sing, they began to enunciate their theology with a fervor that theology often seems to lack. The hymns would provide a way to express the intensity of their new experience, an outlet for a joy they had never before known and hardly knew how to express.

Luccock and Hutchinson saw the Methodist revival as "a singing revival. The Methodists were happy folk. They sang at meeting, on the way to meeting, on the way home from meeting, at home, at work, at leisure. In fact, that was one of the charges sometimes brought against them—that they sang too much."[7] If the people weren't singing with enthusiasm, John and Charles felt something was wrong and set out to find what was out of order.

It didn't take long for John and Charles to begin making their hymns available to all. In 1739, a year after their key religious experiences, they published *Hymns and Sacred Poems*. In total, John published some 64 different hymnals, and in 36, the hymns were entirely the work of John and Charles—and dominantly Charles. John didn't hesitate to edit Charles's hymns, but he allowed no one else to do so. To the best we know, Charles wrote fully 8,989 religious poems, about 6,500 of which can be considered hymns. It's no wonder that someone has said that Charles was a compulsive hymnwriter. Once when he was thrown from a horse (he was never the horseman John was) and suffered from what was probably a concussion, he complained that he wasn't able to write a hymn for two whole days.

Charles wrote his poetry for all sorts of occasions and often for particular individuals. He wrote a hymn "For One in Prison" and another to be sung after "Deliverance from Shipwreck." There were hymns for family life: "For a Woman in Travail," and also, happily, "Thanksgiving for

Her Safe Delivery." Hymns, of course, for the baptism of a child, but also one titled for "A Child When Teething." And farther along in the human story, "At Sending a Child to Boarding School."

I list these titles because I am impressed by the way the hymns took all of life conquest for Christ. No event was too ordinary to be celebrated with a song, no sorrow too small, and no event too mundane. If our Lord said that God notes the sparrow's fall, Charles Wesley's hymns made clear that believers could rightly embrace all of life in the message of their hymn book. In my mind, this does not trivialize the gospel; rather, it brings sacredness to our common life. I'm certain that we would see life in a different way if we would thus bring all of it under the domain of God's love and God's justice.

I submit that two factors were characteristic of Methodist hymnody. One was its emphasis on Jesus Christ. Some theologians have criticized Charles Wesley for not writing more about God. In truth, Wesley put the face of Christ on God, as Christian theology does. In several instances, he uses the phrase "Jehovah crucified"—thus dramatizing God's involvement in the atoning sacrifice of Jesus Christ. I especially like Wesley's description of the incarnation with the daring figure of speech, "Our God contracted to a span."[8] At such times, we see Charles Wesley as not only a theologian but also as a theologian with the gifts of a poet and a dramatist, gifts theologians don't always enjoy.

One of the most powerfully dramatic of Wesley's hymns, "Arise, My Soul, Arise," traces the journey of a soul plagued by "guilty fears." Wesley reminds such a soul that the "bleeding Sacrifice" is appearing before God in his or her behalf: "Before the throne my surety stands. / My name is written on his hands." The hymn ends triumphantly, "With confidence I now draw nigh, / And Father, Abba, Father, cry!"[9] Here are words for a struggling soul. Both John and Charles knew what it was to wrestle with doubts, fears, and assorted terrors, and both were gracious to leave a witness for fellow believers—Charles in his poetry and John in his journal and sermons.

Which leads us to the other particular characteristic of the early Methodist hymns. They are packed full of personal witness. Luccock and Hutchinson compared the hymns of Isaac Watts, William Cowper, Joseph Addison, and Philip Doddridge with those of Charles Wesley, and noted that the quality of the poetry in the others was the equal of Wesley's and, in some cases, superior. What was the secret power of Charles Wesley's hymns? " . . . the pronouns. Wesley started the Methodists singing personal pronouns, and that was what made his hymns a turning point in English history."[10]

Here are some examples:. "O for a thousand tongues to sing / *my* great Redeemer's praise." "A charge to keep *I* have." "Jesus, Lover of *my* soul." "Arise, *my* soul, arise." "And are *we* yet alive?" I am not praising self-centeredness; in contrast, these hymns so often are confessions of need and failure. The power is in the *personal* quality. These Methodist hymns were a testimony service set to music. They were the apostle Paul declaring, "I know whom I have believed" (2 Timothy 1:12, KJV). They are in the spirit of the Psalms, which live and die by the first-person singular. The authority of their belief is not secondhand; it comes from personal experience. Methodism is experiential religion, and the hymns are not ashamed to declare it.

These hymns are saturated with Scripture. For some centuries, the music was almost entirely from the Psalms, careful quotations, or recasting of Scripture. Isaac Watts then opened the door to another kind—a powerful kind!—of hymnody, still centered in Scripture. But no one wove the language and the teachings of Scripture into hymns better than Charles Wesley. I don't know who first said it, but one of the most popular statements about Wesley's hymns is that if the Bible were somehow taken out of our world, we could recover most of it through Charles Wesley's hymns. In fact, as Bernard Manning has pointed out, only four of the thirty-nine Old Testament books and one of the twenty-seven New Testament books are not somewhere quoted in Wesley's hymns. There are more than thirty references to the eighth chapter of Romans alone. Significantly, Wesley's use of Scripture is not simply wholesale quoting or putting verses to music; it is Scripture in action, asserting its place in daily life.

Next to the importance of Scripture is the believers' need to know what they believe; that is, to understand the basics of Christian doctrine. This is especially true for those of us in noncatechetical churches—and desperately true for those churches that no longer include even the formality of a confession of faith at some point in the service of worship. The soul abhors a vacuum, and a religious body that doesn't give its people a system of doctrine will find in time that the secular culture or a conglomerate of heresies has filled the void.

The first Methodists sang their faith, probably without even knowing it. The hymns were full of doctrine, sometimes in direct language and more often by allusion. When I hear Charles Wesley's carol, "Hark, the Herald Angels Sing," in a store at Christmas time, I calculate that there's enough doctrine there to prepare the soul for conversion and for further growth in faith. Consider the second verse: "Christ, by highest heaven adored, / Christ, the everlasting Lord, / late in time behold him come, / offspring of a virgin's womb. / Veiled in flesh the Godhead see; / hail th' incarnate Deity, / pleased with us in flesh to dwell, / Jesus, our Emmanuel."[11] See this triumphant conclusion in verse three: "Mild he lays his glory by, / born that we no more may die, / born to raise us from the earth, / born to give us second birth." An industrious pastor has at least two years of Advent sermons in these lines. And what Wesley did for Advent and Christmas he did for the full church calendar, undergirding the calendar's ability to teach the faith by its very structure.

This emphasis on doctrine was not an accident. John Wesley described his brother's hymns as "a little body of experimental and practical divinity," and he made clear what he meant in a Preface to the *Hymn Book* of 1780 when Methodism was in its second or third generation and when doctrinal clarity was more important than ever.

> In what other publication of the kind have you so distinct and full an account of scriptural Christianity? Such a declaration of the heights and depths of religion, speculative and practical? So strong cautions against the most plausible errors, particularly that are now most prevalent? And so clear directions for making our calling and election sure, for perfecting holiness in the fear of God?[12]

I am cautious about vast, encompassing statements, yet I dare to say that it has been some time since the average church member's knowledge of Christian doctrine has been as vague as it is today. We need these hymns whose allusions awaken our curiosity and whose phrases are an orthodox foundation for Christian belief and for effective daily living.

This, for those hearty Methodists, was the goal of the story. Heaven, yes, but also effective, godly living on this earth. So they sang and so they endeavored:

> To serve the present age,
>   My calling to fulfill;
> O may it all my powers engage
> To do my Master's will![13]

The Methodists knew they were called by God to pursue godly living in their own lives and to bring a better world for this "present age." It was the most practical way to live and so beautiful that you wanted to sing about it.

Back to Andrew Fletcher of Saltoun. He knew that the ballads people sing shape their world more than the laws the legislatures pass. It is still true, which may either frighten or encourage you, depending on how you feel about popular music and our state and federal governments. For me, the issue begins in the church; not because I'm unconcerned about popular culture and politics but because I believe that true biblical living is the greatest gift the church can give to its time. And not because we pass laws to enforce our convictions on others, but because we live with such grace that people are drawn to the same kind of living.

The effectiveness of the church is also shaped by our "ballads." What we sing determines the kind of believers we will become. I have my opinions about the current state of church singing, but I realize that any judgment is still premature; we won't know until perhaps fifty years from now whether our music has been constructive or destructive.

We do know, however, that singing was a key element in the Methodist revival in the British Isles and that it continued with equal force in America for quite some time—long enough and significantly enough that "sing like a Methodist" became a figure of speech in our common language.

In too many instances, we have lost our song or are in process of doing so. You see, it's hard to fool a song. We may sing the same grand words that the redeemed candle makers, street thieves, butchers, and harlots sang two hundred years ago:

> He breaks the power of cancelled sin,
> He sets the prisoners free; . . .[14]

And,

> To serve the present age,
> My calling to fulfill. . . .[15]

I have the painful feeling that modern singers mouth what the early Methodists *souled*. And you can't fool a song.[16] We need to get about the business of gaining the faith that gives the song, after which the song will inform, empower, and excite the faith.

Chapter 9

HOW METHODISM BECAME

AMERICA'S CHURCH

The land we now call America was more than 150 years old when the movement called Methodism began to organize on America's shores. The Episcopal Church (Anglicans) came to America with the Jamestown settlement in 1606, and the Reformed bodies, including what became Presbyterians, Congregationalists, and some groups identified by their national origins, could date themselves to Plymouth Rock in 1620. Roger Williams established a Baptist congregation in Rhode Island in 1638. There were

Jewish congregations in the colonies as early as 1654 and Quakers in Pennsylvania beginning in 1682. Roman Catholics had an early base in Maryland when Lord Baltimore, a faithful Catholic, established the colony and sought in 1649 to make it hospitable to all Christian bodies.

Methodism didn't even exist in the 1600s, and even after it came to birth at Aldersgate, London, in 1738, there was no thought of missions in other parts of the world, especially because Methodism saw itself at first as primarily a renewal movement within the state church in England. A few Methodists immigrated to the colonies, however, and around 1760, an immigrant farmer, Robert Strawbridge, organized meetings in Maryland and Virginia. In 1766, Philip Embury and his cousin, Barbara Heck, began a lay ministry in New York. The next year, the colorful Captain Thomas Webb started a work in Philadelphia. Then, in 1769, as John Wesley recognized both the need and the opportunity in America, he sent Richard Boardman and Joseph Pilmore to the new land and, two years later, Francis Asbury and Richard Wright. At that time, 1771, there were probably six hundred Methodists in all of the colonies with no organization relating the several small local bodies to one another.

Then the smoldering fires of the American Revolution pretty well drove even those few Methodists underground. Methodists were seen, as were the Anglicans, as possible outposts for England and the king, and John Wesley didn't help matters in 1775 by his pamphlet, *A Calm Address to Our*

American Colonies, a work Wesley built largely on Samuel Johnson's *Taxation No Tyranny*. A great many Americans were in no mood to receive counsel from a British clergyman, not even John Wesley. Except for Francis Asbury, all of the preachers Wesley had sent to America returned to England by 1777.

Regardless of such an unpretentious and fumbling start, Methodism survived. Less than a month after George Washington's inauguration as the first President of the new United States of America, four earnest clergy made an official visit: the two bishops of the new Methodist Episcopal Church and two of their leading clergy. These four Methodists were the first religious delegation to recognize formally the new government and its president and to offer blessing to the new nation and its officers.

It was as if the youngest and probably smallest religious body in the new nation had decided that it was their calling before God to begin taking the nation for Christ and for scriptural holiness. Jesse Lee, Methodism's first American historian, put it this way: "The Revolutionary War being now closed, and a general peace established, we could go into all parts of the country without fear; and we soon began to enlarge our borders, and to preach in many places where we had not been before."[1]

What followed is the stuff of history, statistics, and legends. The secret was the preacher on horseback and the driving force a belief that Methodism should reach every part of the nation for God. Someone playfully described it this way: when there were no paths through the wilderness, the Baptist farmer-preachers offered services for their own neighbors. When a horse could break through the wilderness, the Methodist circuit riders came. With the coming of the railroads, the Presbyterian clergy arrived. And when the railroads got Pullman cars, the Episcopalians followed. According to one story, perhaps apocryphal in its details but in general terms no doubt true, a Methodist circuit rider came upon a new settler who was struggling to break the virgin soil. When the circuit rider introduced himself, the farmer threw down his spade in disgust. "I moved out to this wilderness to escape you Methodist preachers!" The circuit rider answered, "Wherever you go in this new land, I promise you there'll soon be a Methodist preacher. If you get to heaven, I'm sure you'll find some there. And if, by dreadful choice, you end in hell, you may even find a Methodist preacher there."

Francis Asbury, America's version of John Wesley, led the way. He led it on horseback, in executive meetings, in vision, in miles traveled, and in tireless preaching. Above all, he led in passion and commitment. Why did he remain in America when all the other British Methodists returned to England? Because, he said, it would be "an eternal dishonor to the Methodist" if they were to leave the souls committed to their care and that "a good shepherd" dare not "leave his flock in time of danger; therefore, I am determined, by the grace of God, not to leave them, let the consequence be what it may."[2]

When American Methodism organized formally at the "Christmas Conference" in Baltimore in 1784, the body received from John Wesley instructions to name Thomas Coke and Francis Asbury as their superintendents. Asbury had somehow grasped the American sense of democracy; he insisted that the Conference itself elect him and Coke rather than simply accepting Wesley's appointment. Their doing so was in its own way their declaration of independence from England. They were a new people governed not by a hereditary ruler, no matter how fine, but by the vote of the body.

The Conference went a step further. They named Coke and Asbury as their bishops thus identifying themselves structurally as "Episcopal" (from the Greek word for bishop) and, therefore, The Methodist Episcopal Church. Wesley was unhappy with their assuming the title of bishop, a term he refused to associate with himself.

For all practical purposes, Asbury became *the* bishop of America. Thomas Coke's heroes were missionaries, and his heart beat for a wide world. He crossed the Atlantic a number of times, gave much leadership to Methodism in Ireland and Wales, and began work in the West Indies. He died while en route to India and was buried at sea. In total, he spent only about three years in America while Asbury traveled the land without pause and, much of the time, without proper rest.

In the more than forty years that Asbury led American Methodism, we can fairly say that he knew America better than any other person in the nation and that no individual was known more widely by the people. He traveled more than 130,000 miles, almost all of it by horseback. Friends and associates urged him to use a carriage more often, but most of the territory he covered had no roads adequate for a carriage. He crossed the Appalachians at least sixty times. He was literally without a home. His mail caught up with him at his stops along the way. When people in England wrote him, addressing letters to "Francis Asbury, America," somehow the letters landed safely in his hands some place in the new nation wherever he happened to be traveling at the time.

Although born and bred as an Englishman, somehow—let us call it the providence of God—he was the quintessential American. Leaving England in 1771, he never returned. He seemed to have an innate sense of democracy though he tended to operate as a dictator. In his sense of democracy, he was a contrast to Thomas Coke, a true English gentleman. In one Conference discussion, Dr. Coke objected to one of the American preachers, Nelson Reed: "You must think you are my equals."[3] Reed answered, "Yes, sir, we do; and we are not only the equals of Dr. Coke but of Dr. Coke's king." This was a new world, indeed, with an attitude regarding the so-called "common man" that was saturating the rough-hewn American clergy and their sometimes even more rough-hewn followers.

Asbury was comfortable with this spirit. As for the vast frontier, he was as at home there as if he had been born in a log cabin. Indeed, if a particular criticism of his leadership and vision can be made, it is that he was not as concerned for ministry to the great, young cities of the east coast as he probably ought to have been. He saw the frontier as the future, and he intended that the Methodist Church would be there to save it for Christ and for civilization.

He had an exhausting task. The growing band of young Methodist preachers had its share of independent personalities, some of whom joined James O'Kelly in a breakaway in 1792 and others who worked at times to get the Methodists to rejoin the Episcopal (Anglican) Church. Asbury couldn't offer many benefits to his preachers. In 1800, for instance, the average annual salary for Congregational ministers was $400 and for Methodists only $80—with many not even paid that meager promise. The majority of the first Methodist preachers had no parsonage because they rode a circuit, covering sometimes hundreds of miles in order to serve all the churches in their charge at least once a month. This meant sleeping in the rough homes of members, often on the floor with their host's children or out in the open. The death rate was predictably high.

Francis Asbury never married, and he openly discouraged his preachers from marrying. After all, it was no life for a wife and children with the preacher-father on the road except for a few days a month. Asbury knew that when a preacher married he would want to "locate" in a city parish where he could serve just one or a few churches, and Asbury felt that Methodism should move to the frontier where the new population was headed.

Asbury's vision worked because so many of his preachers believed as fiercely as he did. Nathan Hatch puts the story in numbers. In 1776, Methodists were less than 3 percent of the church members in America, and in 1850, they were 34 percent—"far and away the largest religious body in the nation and the most extensive national institution other than the Federal government."[4]

Success is pleasant, but it poses problems of its own, especially because success means power and power is usually in conflict with such Christian virtues as humility. John Wesley had sensed this danger very early. "I am not afraid that the people called Methodists should ever cease to exist either in Europe or America. But I am afraid that they should only exist as a dead sect, having the form of religion without the power. And this undoubtedly will be the case unless they hold fast both the doctrines, spirit and disciplines with which they first set out."[5] The statistics themselves were intoxicating, and with the numbers came the feeling of power. Professor Robert D. Clark speaks of "the amazing transition" of a movement "which, in 1830, disdained politics and preached only a simple theology of salvation or damnation, to a denomination that, in 1870, was proud of its political influence,"[6] as reflected especially in its leading bishop at the time, Matthew Simpson.

Eventually Bishop Simpson was the friend of Presidents Lincoln, Grant, and Hayes. His influence with President Lincoln was particularly significant. He was early in urging the emancipation of the slaves, but there is no sure evidence that he played a unique part in the Emancipation Proclamation as is sometimes suggested.

By the time of the Civil War, Methodism's role in the nation was easy to see. Like the Baptists and Presbyterians, Methodism had split over the slavery issue, a division that would not be healed officially until 1939. In 1864, Northern Methodism's General Conference passed a series of resolutions in support of the government and promising the President and his officers their "never-ceasing prayers." When the delegation presented the document to President Lincoln, he responded gratefully. The Methodists had kept thousands of citizens in the border states in the Union, a matter for which Mr. Lincoln had reason to be grateful. He had seen the document before it was officially given to him, so he had prepared a written response. It was politically cautious, noting that the government had been "nobly sustained" by all the churches. Nevertheless, the Methodist Episcopal Church "by its greater numbers, [is] the most important of all. . . . It is no fault in others that the Methodist Church sends more soldiers to the field, more nurses to the hospitals, and more prayers to Heaven than any. God Bless the Methodist Church—bless all the churches—and blessed be God, who, in this our great trial, giveth us the churches."[7] It was not surprising that, when President Lincoln was assassinated, it was Bishop Simpson who offered the prayer at the White House service and who preached the memorial service at Springfield, Illinois.

Methodism's influence now turned in other directions. In 1874, an Ohio inventor, Lewis Miller, and a Methodist Episcopal minister, John Heyl Vincent (eventually to become a bishop), began a new venture in education, faith, culture, and recreation on the shores of Lake Chautauqua in upstate New York. Camp meetings had been in existence in a number of Protestant bodies for more than half a century, but this was a new idea: a place where families could come in the summer to hear great music, see fine drama, learn from key educational and political leaders, in a setting dedicated to religious faith.

Chautauqua got a public relations boost the following year when then-President Ulysses S. Grant visited the grounds. In all, nine American presidents have spoken on the grounds. Franklin Delano Roosevelt chose Chautauqua for what is one of history's most notable presidential speeches, his "I Hate War" address in August, 1936. By that time, however, the name "Chautauqua" had its own kind of magic. In a wide variety of places, Methodists had established other summer settlements, usually on a lake, that they described as "little Chautauquas," and from 1903 to 1930, a number of traveling groups with no tie to Chautauqua took its name for their tent shows—a combination of lectures, concerts, and recitals that entertained in hundreds of small towns and cities of America.

The Chautauqua idea was emblematic of Methodism's attempts to reach the widest possible audience with both faith and learning—the same kind of vision John Wesley demonstrated in writing his dictionary and his more accessible versions of classics for the first generation of Methodists. In America, it also meant the founding of a wide variety of educational institutions, beginning with Cokesbury College. All told, American Methodism has established more than 1,200 schools, colleges, universities, and theological seminaries, of which 124 currently remain. No doubt many of these schools were noble dreams, the vision of earnest lay people and clergy who wanted their community to have a school where their young people could get a fine education in a setting of faith.

These Methodist efforts often led the way. In 1839, the Methodist Episcopal Church founded Wesleyan Female College in Macon, Georgia, the first women's college in the world to grant the B.A. degree. In 1892, in an effort to establish educational standards for its institutions, Methodism created its University Senate. As Professor Kenneth Kinghorn has noted, this was the first accrediting body of its kind in the United States, predating America's regional accrediting organizations. The Chautauqua Institution exhibited the same passion for accessible learning when it began its Literary and Scientific Circle in 1878, a disciplined program of home reading—"for people who never entered high school or college, for merchants, mechanics, apprentices, mothers, busy housekeepers, farmer-boys, shop-girls, and for people of leisure and wealth who do not know what to do with their time."[8] It is one of the oldest if not the first American correspondence school.

Edgar J. Helms, a nineteenth-century Methodist minister in Boston, Massachusetts, used his vision to meet a different kind of need. When an economic depression left many of his parishioners out of work, he conceived of a quite simple, quite brilliant idea: collect used articles of clothing and household items, employ the unemployed to repair them and to sell them—first through church rooms and eventually through independent stores. This was the beginning of Goodwill Industries of America, now operating in 169 cities in the United States and some thirty other countries, though now independent of the Methodist Church.

One would need a master social historian and statistician to find all the institutions—national, international, and local—that began, like the Goodwill Industries, as a Methodist effort and eventually became either interdenominational or secular in its continuing operation. This list would include numerous colleges and universities, hospitals, homes for the aging, adoption programs, orphanages, rescue missions, study programs—as the saying goes, "you name it."

The apostle Paul urged the first generation of believers to "be ready for every good work" (Titus 3:1, NRSV). John Wesley urged Methodists, "Do all the good you can . . . to all the people you can, As long as ever you can,"[9] and the Methodists in America tried to obey both Paul and Wesley. In the process, and as a result of their passion, they became, in the eyes of many, America's church.

Statistically, the Roman Catholic Church might well be seen as America's church today, but Methodism's presence is still the most widespread, with only a handful of counties in the fifty states where there is no United Methodist church. It is an inspiring story of tireless frontier preachers and passionate evangelists. It is a challenge to the church in the twenty-first century.

Chapter 10

METHODISM AND HER
SEVERAL CHILDREN

Religious movements of every kind tend to multiply by division. In the Muslim world, one thinks of the Shiites and Sunnis. American Judaism has its Orthodox, Conservative, and Liberal bodies. The Eastern Orthodox Church has bodies that identify themselves by their particular ethnic roots. Roman Catholicism experienced its greatest divisions during the period of the Protestant Reformation, when Lutheranism, Calvinism, and, later, Anglicanism broke away. As an outside observer, I sometimes admire the

Catholic Church for holding onto some distinct subidentities by way of its Orders—Franciscans, Benedictines, and Jesuits, for example—which in Protestantism might have become separate denominations.

Then there is Methodism. When I refer to Methodism's "several children," I'm treating the matter positively, and I should note quickly that these children seem always to leave home, sometimes as organized or semiorganized movements and other times as individuals who then coalesce into other movements.

I believe deeply in cooperation and the spirit of goodwill, but I am not unduly upset with the general tendency in religion toward division. When we humans possess vigorous convictions about a subject, we're susceptible to division. People who have no particularly strong convictions see no reason to leave, to reform, or to renew. It is unfortunate and indeed un-Christian when those strong convictions cause people to become hateful toward others and to consign them to hell, or to description by adjectives of scorn and contempt. On the other hand, an institution—whether religious, political or social—that has no deep feelings can slowly die of its own weight and boredom. I dare to think, therefore, that though religious dissension is sometimes an expression of ego-centered leaders or a tendency to make major causes out of minor issues, they spring from life and not from weariness and indifference.

John Wesley, the primary founder of Methodism, was a strong and autocratic leader. He would have been a notable leader if he had gone into politics or industry. I think one of the most admirable facts about his person is that he didn't confuse himself with God nor did he exploit the Methodist movement for personal economic gain or ego satisfaction. Human beings don't cease to be human because they have devoted themselves to God; they are still susceptible to a variety of temptations, including the intoxication of power. I submit that, on the whole, John Wesley handled power with a remarkable degree of true piety.

It was not always so. During Wesley's brief stay in Georgia, he was sometimes a religious tyrant, for example refusing to serve communion to a bishop of the Moravian body. It's surprising that this trait didn't show itself more dangerously in the years following when Wesley had almost unlimited power as the leader of the Methodist movement. As he himself wrote during one controversy, his preachers "had no power at all, but what I exercised through them."[1] The holiness that Wesley preached clearly was at work in his own life, and he became more tolerant with age. He wrote to a young Anglican preacher, "The longer I live, the larger allowances I make for human infirmities. I exact more from myself, and less from others."[2] This is a good rule for any leader.

When America became an independent nation, Wesley recognized that the Methodists in America must also become independent. He didn't expect them to become as quickly and vigorously independent of his own leadership as they did at the Christmas Conference, but he was wise enough not to get in their way.

Francis Asbury, who imbibed the spirit of democracy on the frontier, was nevertheless a single-minded leader and a demanding one. He disciplined himself with an iron hand and expected others to be equally demanding of themselves. The presiding elders who worked with him, essentially as district superintendents work today with a bishop, learned that they would have little voice in the process of appointing pastors to churches. When people made suggestions, Asbury feared that their judgments were influenced by their prejudices, hardly recognizing that he might have prejudices of his own.

He was generally sustained by the high regard in which both preachers and lay people held him. But there were often murmurings, and in time, the murmuring became an exodus led by one of the brightest young preachers, James O'Kelly. O'Kelly argued that, after a bishop had made appointments, a preacher who felt he had been wronged should be able to appeal to the Conference, and the Conference have the power to overrule the appointment. The Virginia Conference debated the issue for three days and eventually voted against O'Kelly's motion. O'Kelly then left the church, and a substantial number followed him, especially in Virginia and North Carolina. The Methodist Episcopal Church was only eight years old at the time, but it recovered rapidly from the loss. Though O'Kelly was a good and able man, his movement slowly went out of existence.

A break came in 1830, however, which gave rise to the Methodist Protestant Church. This movement, like O'Kelly's, was a call for more democracy within the church. Particularly, the Methodist Protestant movement insisted on lay representation in the ruling bodies of the denomination, along with the clergy. The parent body eventually saw the wisdom of this idea, but it was long after the group had pulled away.

A significant exodus came in 1843. This movement was led by both clergy and lay people who were strongly opposed to slavery and who were troubled that the Methodist Episcopal Church was not acting decisively enough in dealing with the issue. When they concluded that their voices were not being heard, twenty-two ministers and 6,000 members left the denomination to become the Wesleyan Methodist Connection of America. They were also troubled by what they saw as abusive use of power by the bishops of the church. Their new body abolished the office, included lay participation in their annual conference, and elected a president instead of a bishop. They also re-emphasized some of the holiness practices they felt were being neglected in the parent body.

In 1947, they changed their name to the Wesleyan Methodist Church, then simply to the Wesleyan Church in 1968 in their merger with the Pilgrim Holiness Church, a

Wesleyan body that had come to birth in the late nineteenth century during the holiness revivals that were affecting so much of America at the time, especially in rural areas and small towns. As of 2010, the Wesleyan Church had 139,000 members in the United States, with 1,716 ordained clergy. Worldwide, they number more than 344,000 members.[3]

The Free Methodist Church of North America was born in 1860, the result of two reform movements within the Methodist Episcopal Church that were unsuccessful. The Genesee Conference of the church expelled Benjamin T. Roberts and several other ministers after their reform movement was rejected. Some lay people, particularly in New York and Illinois, agreed with Roberts and his colleagues and joined with them in the new body. They added "Free" to their name because of their emphasis on free pews, freedom for slaves, and freedom in worship. They gave renewed emphasis to the doctrine of entire sanctification. They also, like the Methodist Protestants, gave an equal role to the laity so that in every decision-making body there would be an equal number of lay and clergy representatives. This denomination is still in existence today, with more than 75,000 members in the United States and 1,053 local congregations.

Methodism's most serious break came of course over the issue of slavery. What Abraham Lincoln said in his Second Inaugural Address of the nation as a whole was surely true of Methodism at the time: "Both read the same Bible and pray to the same God, and each invokes His aid against the other."[4] In any event, Methodist churches in the South broke from the parent body in 1844 and became the Methodist Episcopal Church South. It was almost a century later, in 1939, that the breach was healed, and the Methodist Episcopal Church, the Methodist Episcopal Church South, and the Methodist Protestant Church became, by merger and reunion, The Methodist Church.

A further merger took place in 1968 when The Methodist Church and the Evangelical United Brethren Church became one. The latter denomination was itself a merger of denominations that were made up originally of German immigrants in America. Their theology was Wesleyan, and when the language barrier ceased to exist as the second generation of families grew, a merger of the bodies seemed altogether logical and has been more than cordial.

Each of these mergers and reunions brought gains to the united body beyond simply the membership itself. Each body had its own schools, children's homes, orphanages, publishing houses, and homes for the aging. Each brought its particular hymnody along with the music that was cherished by all three, and each brought unique strengths in programs for youth, women, and men. Each also brought its own quality of piety and particular characteristics of worship, though sometimes the differences were noticeable only to those who were deeply entrenched in a particular heritage. No matter; there was a general enriching through the union.

There were losses too. Because it was a much smaller body, the Evangelical United Brethren had a sense of personal investment in its mission programs, its schools, and other institutions that gradually was lost. Some leaders in both denominations had hoped that perhaps the smaller body would bring a kind of spiritual leaven to the merger, adding vitality to the larger body. The substantial difference in size limited such influence.

It was also the case in both 1939 and 1968 that some congregations and leaders refused to join the mergers. Thus we have today the Southern Methodist Church and the Evangelical Methodist Church, as well as some local congregations that simply claimed their own independence when they found themselves unwilling to join the merger of their parent bodies.

Several of the most significant Wesleyan bodies also came into existence by way of America's history of slavery. The story is at times beautiful and at times sad. One encounters both nobility of spirit and narrowness of spirit. Richard Allen was born into slavery in Philadelphia in February 1760. At seventeen, he was converted and began preaching, both at the plantation and in local Methodist churches. His owner was one of his first converts. Impressed by Allen's ability and his faith, his owner allowed him to purchase his freedom.

Allen soon was preaching in Methodist circuits through Delaware and adjoining states. Bishop Asbury and other Methodist preachers helped arrange preaching engagements.

In 1786, Allen joined St. George's Methodist Church. It was primarily a white congregation with a few African members. With Allen's influence, more Africans began to join, the congregation became roiled on issues of seating and the use of the altar, so Richard Allen and a fellow former slave, Absalom Jones, left the church with fellow Africans and formed a new congregation.

In time, Jones became Episcopalian, and Richard Allen, feeling that his people needed their own identity, established the Bethel African Methodist Episcopal Church. Bishop Francis Asbury led the service of dedication and ordained Allen a deacon. In April 1816, Allen and a number of other African American leaders established the African Methodist Episcopal Church (AMEC), and Bishop Asbury consecrated Allen as the first bishop of the church. They adopted the Twenty-Five Articles of the Methodist Episcopal Church, its General Rules, and the episcopal system of government. Allen sought especially, however, to focus on "a pious, moral life" for his people. According to the World Christian Database, in 2010, the African Methodist Episcopal Church had 2,697,000 members in 8,915 churches. Their AME Book Concern was the first publishing house owned and operated by African Americans, and in 1847, they began a weekly magazine, later to be known as *The Christian Recorder*, which is the oldest African American magazine published by African Americans.

The African Methodist Episcopal Zion Church has a somewhat similar story of rejection and determination. In 1796, four African American members of the John's Street Methodist Episcopal Church in New York City grew weary of being discriminated against; they were not allowed to preach or to vote in church conferences and led a group of fellow African Americans out of the congregation. Led by James Varick, they petitioned Bishop Asbury to have their own meetings, and Bishop Asbury agreed.

After a period of years and a series of struggles, in June 1821, nineteen African American preachers organized the African Methodist Episcopal Zion Church (AMEZC) and chose Varick as their first bishop. Like the AMEC, they adopted the ritual and doctrines of the Methodist Episcopal Church as spelled out in the Twenty-Five Articles of Religion. In 2010, their body included 3,305 churches in the United States with 1,596,000 members.

Following the Civil War, the remaining African American members of the Methodist Episcopal Church South chose not to join the AMEC or the AMEZC, but with the help of their former masters, they established a separate denomination and gained title of their church property from white trustees and formed the Colored Methodist Episcopal Church (CMEC). In time, they expanded into the northern and western states. The body changed its name to the Christian Methodist Episcopal Church in 1954. Its membership in 2010 was listed as 919,000 persons in 3,592 local churches.

One of the best known religious bodies in the world is the Salvation Army, though great numbers of persons have no idea that it is a religious body and even fewer know that its roots are in Methodism. In some ways, however, perhaps no religious body in the twenty-first century—including The United Methodist Church—comes closer to John Wesley's teaching and practice of personal and social holiness.

William Booth was a Methodist minister in England, but as he and his wife Catherine became increasingly concerned for the most lost and disadvantaged of London's poor, they broke from their parent Methodist body in 1865, at first under the name of the Christian Mission. In 1878, they changed their name to the Salvation Army and took upon themselves patterns of structure, dress, titles, and discipline that characterized their war against sin and hell. Many who know little or nothing of their religious convictions know simply that wherever there is human need, the Salvation Army is likely to be the first on the scene.

As we have noted several times, Methodism was born as a renewal movement rather than as a reforming body. That quality showed itself in two significant movements within Protestant America in the mid- and late nineteenth and early twentieth centuries and continues into the twenty-first century. The first was the holiness revival and the second the Pentecostal movement. Neither was exclusively Methodist, by any means. Several of the most effective leaders in the nineteenth century holiness movement, for example, were Quakers, and a number of Baptists were among the Pentecostal pioneers.

The Methodists offered hospitable ground for those with a heart for renewal. For one thing, beginning with Charles and John Wesley in May 1738, there had been an emphasis on religious experience. Methodism believed from the start that Christianity is not simply a body of doctrine, nor is it perceived only by intellectual persuasion, but it is also a matter of heart and emotion. Renewal movements spring from deep conviction, and while those convictions may be logical and reasoned-through, they are likely to find their energy in emotion.

Also, renewal depends on a base of support in lay people. In such movements, it is often difficult to distinguish between the ordained clergy and the zealous lay person. In many instances, the lay person may be more eloquent in expression than the trained homiletician. This was true of Methodism from its beginning. Wesley's first aides came from laborers and tradesmen, servants, and waiting girls. As we noted earlier, Methodism got its start in America in lay people like Philip Embury, Barbara Heck, Captain Thomas Webb, and Robert Strawbridge before John Wesley had sent preachers to the new land. Whatever was left of that quality in American Methodism provided good seed ground for the holiness and Pentecostal movements.

The holiness movement of the nineteenth century quite naturally began among Methodists because this was a basic teaching of the Wesley brothers in both sermon and song. Thus those groups that broke from the parent body, like the Wesleyan Methodists and the Free Methodists, were quite right in retaining "Methodist" in their name. No doubt they claimed better right to the name than some whom they saw as departing from the original faith. Phineas Brezee, a Methodist Episcopal minister, was a key to the founding of the Church of the Nazarene, which became a major holiness body.

The holiness revivals came to have a life of their own, starting sometimes with individuals in small communities that then became local churches and, in some instances, forming small, usually regional denominations. Some were the result of dynamic leaders like Hannah Whitall Smith, a Quaker, and Phoebe Palmer, a Methodist. Both influenced thousands upon thousands in America and abroad.

The Pentecostal movement had its beginnings with persons of a number of denominations as well as those with no clear affiliation, but Methodists were prominent in the early days of the movement. For some, the Pentecostal experience seemed simply an extension of the perfection they had always sought, while for others it was a new experience of power and zeal.

One way and another, Methodism has spread to literally every part of the world. Thus when the World Methodist Council meets every five years, there is a parade of flags and costumes from 111 different Methodist bodies throughout the world. These bodies now claim more than 75 million members and adherents. When John Wesley declared, "The world is my parish," he was defending himself against the charge that he had no established preaching place, so he would be at home anywhere he might declare his faith. Today his declaration can be measured by statistics and by locations on every part of the globe.

Obviously the Methodist family, under a variety of names and a host of flags, is bigger than John and Charles could ever have imagined. And to think that its roots were in a rectory in little Epworth, England!

Chapter 11

METHODISM TODAY

I t is an exciting story. Two boys who grew up in an inland English village nearly three centuries ago started something that now influences people around the world. Millions still sing the songs Charles Wesley wrote, and millions still identify themselves with John Wesley's theology, albeit sometimes with rather vague attachments. These two men and others close to them wanted to see a revitalizing, a kind of rebirth, of the Christian faith as they knew it. They saw it happen in their lifetime in their homeland in greater measure and activity and variety of expression than they could ever have imagined. Half a century after their deaths, the movement they started was the single most significant religious body in the new nation of America.

Religious revivals in the Christian community generally become history within a generation; "God has no grandchildren," as some unknown evangelist once put it. Usually the best a second generation can offer is thoughtful studies of the previous generation or sentimental yearning for what once was. The Methodist movement defied that pattern while hardly realizing it was doing so. As we have noted earlier, John Wesley feared that Methodism would continue as an institution while losing its vitality, but the movement was well into its second generation before John's death and was still growing numerically and with faithful application of its commitment to personal and social holiness. Nearly two generations later, when it appeared British Methodism was settling into comfortable middle age, it was vigorously born again in the Salvation Army, under the midwifery of William and Catherine Booth, and this time with drums, trumpets, and uniforms.

As for America, while the Methodist revival was still at its best in England, Ireland, and Wales, it survived the trip overseas and against a variety of odds made itself at home in the new nation. In America, the mission was not the renewal of the Anglican Church or of any other established religious body; rather, it was the conversion of a nation with the special mission of saving a frontier from the moral, social, and intellectual perils that the westward expansion threatened.

While some of the early ardor may have diminished somewhat, the denomination continued to grow in America. At times, the motivation for growth may have seemed more like enthusiasm for a social club, but there were enough memories of yesterday's faith to bring fervor to the membership drives of the new generation.

Who can measure the broad impact of the Methodist movement? What has been its influence beyond hymns and prayer meetings and the sacraments? Jesus described his followers as salt and leaven and light in their larger world. Has Methodism been significant by that measure?

More than one historian has made a case for Methodism's wider influence in eighteenth-century England. As we have noted earlier, the time of Methodism's birth was a period of great economic and social ferment. Industrialization was an irresistible force, with fallout that could easily have destroyed the best of the human dream. The French historian, Elie Halevy, reasons that the volatile potential of the British economic and social order in the eighteenth century made it susceptible to anarchy and that Methodism and the evangelical movement saved England from the kind of revolution that shook France in the last decade of that same century. Obviously, other elements were also at work, but Halevy's case is impressive. Another thoughtful analyst, Robert Wearmouth, showed in his research that British Methodism trained large numbers of the nation's working classes in arts of leadership and in the methods of a disciplined movement that strongly influenced British political and economic life for several generations to come.

As for Methodism's wider influence in American life, let me say a further word about how basic Methodist theology fit the spirit of the new country in its first generation as a nation and how in turn it helped shape the nation. Much of the Protestant theology of the Pilgrims and their immediate successors was Calvinist, which emphasized that God had chosen those who would be saved and those who would be damned. Methodism insisted vigorously that God's salvation was for all humanity, for anyone—underline *anyone*—could be saved because Christ had died for all.

It is not surprising that this theology captured a country that was just coming to birth with all of its new ideals of the worth of every person. Nor is it surprising that Methodism appealed so much to the African American slaves and that some of their early preachers were nurtured, encouraged, and promoted by Bishop Francis Asbury. While the American Constitution, as originally approved, made the slave three-fifths of a person, a gospel that said Christ died for all gave the slave a rightful dignity, even if legislatures and the culture were slow to grant it.

So, too, with Methodism's leadership in woman's suffrage. Women had a vote in Methodist General Conference sessions nearly a generation before the Nineteenth Amendment to the Constitution. And so, too, with Methodism's call for social equality in "The Social Creed of the Methodist Episcopal Church," which the General Conference of the church passed in 1908. A few months later, thirty-three Protestant denominations formed the Federal Council of the Churches of Christ in America and adopted the Methodist statement almost word for word as "The Social Creed of the Churches." So much of what we take for granted as the democratic spirit of America was nurtured and sometimes implemented by the Methodist movement. Mind you, it was never a story of even progress and never without its embarrassing inconsistencies and aberrations, but no human project ever is.

This, then, is the Methodist story. I repeat, it is an exciting story and compelling in its character and its influence. But where is Methodism today?

It depends on where you look. If you're in Korea, where thousands gather in huge buildings each Sunday and hundreds hurry early in the morning every weekday for an hour of prayer before going to their day's work, you will conclude that Methodism is as healthy as it was in the best days of Wesley and Asbury. If you gather statistics from The United Methodist Church in many countries of Africa, you will discover that the figures will be outdated before you have them in print. New churches are coming to birth week after week, and established congregations are growing steadily. Methodism is alive and well and laying hold of the future for the Kingdom of God.

There are congregations in America where the quality of worship, the sense of mission, the commitment to social and spiritual service, and the numerical growth of the congregation all give living evidence that the future is bright. Whatever is ahead, such churches seem ready to meet it. One thinks immediately of certain landmark churches where not only hundreds or even several thousand are in attendance on the weekend but where programs of learning, service, outreach, and spiritual growth also occur all through the week. There are also such stories on a smaller scale, some of them in medium size vital congregations, gladly filling their place in all kinds of communities. I know also of rural and village churches that, a few years ago, had only eight or ten persons in church on any given Sunday where now they number fifty or one hundred, and there is excitement about the future.

But this isn't the common story statistically or anecdotally. For one thing, we know that vast numbers of United Methodists—probably a majority—know little of their denomination's history and the reasons to recall it with pride. They probably know even less about Christian doctrine in general and about Methodist doctrine in particular. Perhaps they have heard on some spring Sunday that that they are celebrating Aldersgate Day, but they have no idea of what this means in the church's history and nothing of its place in Methodist doctrine or what significance it might hold for their own Christian experience. Quite honestly, there is little reason to remain a Methodist and still less reason to encourage others to become Methodists if one knows nothing about the church and its teachings that give one reason for worthy pride and for the difference that Methodism might bring to everyday life.

It is popular just now to say that "all religions are alike," a statement that is as much of an insult to an earnest advocate of another faith as it is an abandonment of one's own. It is one thing, and a very bad thing, to be condescending or scornful of the beliefs of other people, and if knowing one's own faith leads to such an attitude, then it is a poor reflection on one's faith. But we should know why we are who we are. Our world is a marketplace of ideas and philosophies of life. If we don't know our Methodist heritage and doctrine, then we are unprepared for a culture where people are making life decisions every day without ever having heard a viable case for following Jesus Christ.

I confess that if twenty-first-century Methodists are to know their identity, then they will be going against the tide of the current culture. Most of the persons in contemporary America who know their spiritual heritage are either members of a small, probably rather isolated religious group or among the comparatively few of the very devout within Catholic, Orthodox and a variety of Protestant congregations. It would be to the benefit of the nation if those who claim religious affiliation were enough in earnest to know their basic doctrines and were true enough to those doctrines to be properly humble in their relationship to those who are different and equally proud of who they are.

The people who first took the name "Methodist" knew who they were and what they believed. In many instances, they were not literate, so they got the message orally. With their salvation came a hunger for learning. As I have indicated earlier, Wesley saw to it that the first Methodists had books—especially religious books, but also books that would add to their general knowledge. Methodism's first preachers in America were not scholars, and living on horseback didn't provide much opportunity for study. Nevertheless, they carried books to the frontier, and the odds were good that a Methodist family would have a Bible and a hymn book and perhaps another book or two from the Methodist Book Concern. And if there were any periodical in the home, then it was likely to be a Methodist magazine or paper.

It is quite a different story today. The Bible and other documents of Christian training have to struggle for a place in the rush of daily life. Even those persons who have taken the vows of United Methodist membership have to be convinced that it is worth their time to learn more about the Bible or about the beliefs of the church to which they belong. The frontier circuit rider had to fight rain, hail, snow, and nearly impassable rivers. The twenty-first-century preacher has to make a path through the wilderness of preoccupied people, whose lives are packed full of television, Internet, community responsibilities, demanding work (or a disheartening search for work), and a daily commute that claims some of life's best energy.

As a longtime pastor, I am quite sure that we clergy should lead the way in encouraging our people to know who they are and why, but I also know that this is a daunting task. Whether one is a religious publisher, trying to produce books, periodicals, or study programs that will meet the needs of this time, a denominational executive assigned the task of invigorating his or her body, or a parish pastor working with fifty or a hundred or five thousand persons: no matter, the task is daunting.

But it is worth trying.

Nobody should know this better than Methodists, a people who came into existence because a few people in eighteenth-century England believed in holy renewal.

So back to the question. Where is Methodism today? It is clear enough that we are not the Methodism of John and Charles Wesley and eighteenth-century field preaching; nor are we the Methodism of Francis Asbury, when the nation was a wilderness to be conquered. Indeed, it is not even the Methodism of my childhood that preceded the reuniting of the Methodist Episcopal, Methodist Protestant, and Methodist Episcopal South into one body, or that in my adult life saw the merger of the Methodist Church and the Evangelical United Brethren Church.

Nor is it the Methodism into which I became a pastor in 1950 where nationally Methodism organized teams of lay people—usually men—to go out an evening each week, two by two, calling on people in their homes to invite them to attendance and membership in the Methodist Church. It was a church that was still growing numerically. At that time, we were not comfortable simply to register numerical growth because we were concerned that our rate of growth wasn't quite keeping up with the growth of the population.

The story is very different now and has been for a long time. The United Methodist Church in this second decade of the twenty-first century is a denomination that has been suffering membership decline every year for more than a generation. Thus it is a denomination with an entire generation of pastors, bishops, and district superintendents who have never known what it is, numerically, to be part of a growing body. Mind you, some individual congregations have grown, but never in a generation has the national body known a net increase in membership.

Someone wants at this point to tell me that things are bad all over, that currently there is no major Christian body in America, other than the Roman Catholic church, that is showing net growth. True. But I'm sure Francis Asbury wouldn't have accepted such a mantra. Asbury would have reasoned that such statistics proved how badly the culture needed the Methodist message and witness. The worse things are, he might have said, the heavier our responsibility to make a difference.

I venture that the biggest challenges facing The United Methodist Church in this second decade of the century is, as it has been for almost a generation, that we are divided and distracted. The most obvious point of division is in our view of homosexual conduct and, with it, our attitude toward the authority of Scripture and our interpretation of Scripture. I'm quite sure that all of us could hear one another better in our discussions of this key issue if we could get the holy humility to listen with more grace and wisdom. Is this possible? I like to believe that with God, all things are possible.

There are distractions. Distraction is the middle name of our culture, and it is as much of an issue in the church as in all of life. Indeed, if the church in our time is to redeem our times, then we will have to be saved from our own distractions so we can heal the distractions of our society. That is, we need to be sure of what is central and what is not—while not forgetting that those things that are not central may still nevertheless be important.

Methodism, as most of us know it, is a movement of *causes*. This is natural to a *whole* gospel. If one believes (as surely a true Methodist would) that Christianity affects all of life, then all of life is important. In a sense, there is no subject or preaching or teaching that is outside the proper concern of the Gospel. From its earliest days, the Methodist movement was concerned about everything: the physical, mental, social, and spiritual well-being of every human being, and thus the economic, political, and social forces that affect each person.

If one believes this, then one is going to be drawn to many issues, concerns, and causes. Probably most of these causes are good, though not always in the way we express them and not necessarily in the amount of attention we give to them. Methodism needs to remember what is first and to keep it first in order that all of those things that are second may also have a chance to survive. If that which is first is neglected, then all else will go down with it. Many persons in the church are called to pursue particular issues with singular devotion; this is their place in the body of Christ. But neither they nor the larger body should confuse them and their cause with that which is first. Most of us know that we should not be distracted by that which is evil. Our greater problem is that we become distracted by that which is good so that we lose sight of that which is crucial.

The United Methodist Church tends these days—like the culture in which it lives—to divide its soul between many causes until it no longer recognizes its own soul. So it is difficult to say where United Methodism is today because United Methodism is not really sure of its own identity. With that issue before us, it is time to ask ourselves about the future.

Chapter 12

WHAT IS THE FUTURE OF METHODISM?

What is the future of Methodism? Particularly, what is the future of The United Methodist Church, the largest single body in Methodism? It can be instructive and even inspiring to talk about the past, but what of the future? Institutions come and go, as do nations and empires. Rudyard Kipling warned Great Britain at a high point in her history, "Lo, all our pomp of yesterday / Is one with Nineveh and Tyre."[1] Is Methodism just an interesting interlude in the history of the church to be forgotten in time except by scholars in the field, or is it a continuing element in God's work of redemption? Does it have a future?

My first response is a personal one—the sort of thing people sometimes declare as a matter of full disclosure. As I look at the teachings of Methodism and its heritage, I ask myself where I would go if there were no United Methodist Church or its Wesleyan equivalent. I have nothing against Presbyterians, Episcopalians, Baptists, Lutherans, etc. I can be at home worshiping in any of these bodies, and some of the preachers I admire most are outside the Methodist fold. I have come to cherish much of what the Catholic Church has given us. But for me, something basic would be missing in any of these other bodies.

You might answer, "It's sentiment. You're not being logical." You have a point but not a compelling one. True; I cut my teeth, as the saying goes, on a Methodist hymn book, and I have a vast and varied collection of Methodist memories. But I've left room for logic, and it's a big room. I believe in the doctrines of Methodism and their solid roots in the Scriptures and the teachings of the early Church. I embrace with my whole being the belief that God's love is all-encompassing, not selective, and that if anyone is left out it is by his or her choice, not God's. I cherish the Methodist conviction that holiness is important and that, if it is to be true holiness, it must be both personal and social. I like Methodism's balance of head and heart, its conviction that what one believes should be intellectually honest and also emotionally satisfying. I believe profoundly that the Christian life is one of untiring growth—a kind of salvation that says one is born again not simply to get into heaven but also to grow up on earth—and that this "growing up" is spiritual, emotional, intellectual, and social until (in the language of the apostle Paul) we are "to be fully grown, measured by the standard of the fullness of Christ" (Ephesians 4:13, CEB).

I admit that you won't find all of the elements I've just described in every United Methodist Church or in every Wesleyan church of other bodies, but this is the Methodist heritage, it is why we came into existence, and it is who we are. I don't have to invent a movement in order to bring together these elements in healthy and exciting balance. The pattern is there, and it has proven itself in thousands of local congregations over several centuries. And there is no reason why it can't be born again in any congregation.

But I realize that I haven't yet answered the question. I've told you what Methodism means to me but the question still remains: does it have a future? When The United Methodist Church has suffered a net loss of several million members over the past forty years and the other Methodist bodies in America have also lost ground or have had no measurable gain, what does the future hold but slow and steady decline? In a social institution, nothing is as difficult as to reverse as a negative trend. After a while, people become so accustomed to the trend that it no longer disturbs them. They become comfortable with loss and failure and spend more time rationalizing their reasons for loss than seeking means of gain.

Some would remind us that we can't measure the work of the church by statistics alone, and of course, they're right. It will always be difficult to calculate the true achievements of the church because so much of what the church seeks to do defies our usual systems of calculation. How do we register the influence of a godly life or the transforming effectiveness of teaching and preaching or the redemptive power of a truly fine human being, the kind of person we think of as a living saint? Who, other than God, can say how many souls are saved, to what degree lives are changed, or how much it means for some broken heart to be mended or some careless person awakened to goodness and purity? The best of what the church does cannot be compiled in records of attendance or in dollars contributed and spent. Nevertheless, we have to pay some attention to these statistics because we can't influence persons unless they're present, in person at best or by means of radio, television, or Internet. The work we seek to do, whether in feeding the poor, healing the sick, or caring for the forgotten requires money—so, yes, statistics do matter, even though they are not the ultimate, eternal measure of the work of the church. To put it mildly, many of the current key statistics in Methodism are not encouraging.

So can the Methodist movement be born again? In a time when the prevalent cliché is, "I'm not religious, but I'm very spiritual," and when the assenting reply is likely to be,

"I love Jesus, but I don't like the church," is it possible for Methodist churches to re-establish themselves as a growing social institution? It is now fully a generation of time that people have been turning away from organizations, all the way from bowling teams to service clubs, labor unions, and secret societies. The church has of course felt this prevailing mood; people don't want to join anything. The growing edge of Christianity seems to be the megachurch where membership is played down. Can typical churches hope to counter the social tide and begin once again to grow in numbers and effectiveness?

Let it be noted that, in two millennia of its history, the church has known other times when the general tide was against growth. It has survived such times in the past and has, in some instances, enjoyed its greatest fruitfulness when the times were incompatible. Indeed, Methodism came to birth at just such a time. For one, there was no need, it seemed, for a new religious body in eighteenth-century England because there was a state church and it was everyone's privilege to belong. To become part of the Methodist renewal movement was, pragmatically, like having two churches; and furthermore, the second was going to cost something because it didn't have the support of the government. It can be said fairly that the masses in eighteenth-century England didn't think well of religion; the odds were decidedly against religious renewal. Who cared, if any?

Nor were the odds good when Methodism came to America. Students of the westward movement note that many of the people who moved to the frontier did so to get away from organizations of any kind; they were happy to keep the government itself at a distance, and their spirit of independence extended to voluntary bodies as well. It was an unlikely time to build churches when the settlers hardly had houses to cover their own heads and barely enough resources to keep alive as they broke virgin soil. A sophisticated sociological study would have told Francis Asbury to retreat, not advance.

So, no, the temper of the times is not a reason to give up. It is, indeed, a reason for evaluating the nature of advance but not an argument for retreat.

John Wesley feared that the Methodists would become a "dead sect" by having lost their "doctrine, spirit, and disciplines with which they first set out."[2] Wesley's statement shows clearly that he considered doctrine to be important and that, if we lost our doctrinal distinction, we had no good reason to continue to exist. But I fear that it would be painful these days to ask any group of Methodists what Methodists believe. It is popular just now, with the increasing population of Muslims, Buddhists, and Hindus for local churches to offer classes in the beliefs of these religions so that their members will understand what their neighbors believe. I think it is altogether possible that many contemporary United Methodists will come out of such an introductory course knowing more about the teachings of their neighbors' religion than they have ever known about their own.

We cannot expect a renewal within United Methodism without an informed laity. A religious body, whatever its name or doctrine, is by its very nature a body of believers. If the people in a body have no idea what they believe and no perception than their beliefs make a difference, then there is no continuing reason for membership in that body. I know that the quality of preaching is important; as a pastor, I worked constantly for such quality, and as a teacher of future preachers, I have tried to persuade my students to pursue excellence. But a church must be more than a winsome pulpit. I sympathize, too, with the need for a good church building with adequate physical facilities, but those who come primarily for the quality of a church's classrooms, parlor, gymnasium, and worship center will shortly turn to something newer and more attractive. So, too, with a church's program, its activities, its community service, its music. Each and all of these are important, but they are not at the core of who we are. The DNA of a religious body lies in its doctrine.

So it is time for any self-respecting religious body to ask itself, "Who are we? Why did we come into existence? Is there any reason for us to continue?" If we have lost our identity and our purpose, then why are we still here? Is it honorable for us to continue if we have no unique reason for existence and if, by our disappearance, the human soul would suffer no loss?

Anyone who came to a Methodist meeting house in eighteenth-century England or nineteenth-century America soon knew what the body believed. Its basic Christian doctrines were profoundly biblical. They were classic; they were the beliefs of the Christian faith as handed down through the centuries. They were not only preached and taught, but they were also sung. John Wesley said that the hymns of Methodism were "a body of practical and experimental theology."[3] The description is itself a declaration of doctrine. Methodism was, from its beginning, a theology of experience and one that lived itself out in daily practice. Early Methodists were likely to know the classic creeds of the church, but if not, they would have the content in the hymns they sang. If there is to be a renewal in Methodism, then it will eventually include a renewed birth of music with content. Faith sung, even by those who sing poorly, is faith with a quality of emotion and conviction.

Which brings us to another key factor. Traditionally, Methodism emphasizes religious experience. John and Charles Wesley knew their doctrine well; they could discuss it in Latin and read its scriptural basis in the original languages of the Scriptures, Hebrew, and Greek. But knowledge alone was not enough. As their father Samuel had said, religion needs "the inner witness."

Most of us are deeply moved when we hear someone tell of his or her conversion from drug usage or alcoholism or a life of crime, but religious experience isn't limited to such dramatic stories. John and Charles Wesley are evidence of that. As far as dramatic sin is concerned, they had lived sheltered lives. They probably knew less personally about such conduct than a majority in a typical twenty-first-century congregation. Nevertheless, they had a conversion experience, one that would cause Charles to write shortly after his experience, "Where shall my wondering soul begin? / How shall I all to heaven aspire? / A slave redeemed from death and sin, / A brand plucked from eternal fire."[4] We don't have to be drug addicts or murderers to know that we need a Savior.

We would do well to give twenty-first-century persons more opportunity to experience their faith and to share their experiences with their fellow worshipers. A sensitive pastor learns that, in every church, there are people who have faith experiences that mean much to them but that they hesitate to mention because they fear they will be seen as odd or fanatical. It is not evidence of poor thinking to speak of religious experience. Blaise Pascal, one of the true geniuses of human history, proved as much by the vigor and depth of his witness. Methodism restored to the church the emphasis on faith experienced as well as religion taught. We have nearly lost this from our churches, and we are desperately poorer because of this loss. Methodism is a faith of head and heart.

We must restore to our churches a belief in and the practice of holiness. Traditional Wesleyan doctrine insists that this is a matter both personal and social. Our holiness should demonstrate itself in how we use our money and our time. It should show itself in our conversation—not only in the language we choose but also in what we talk about. I am not suggesting that all of Christian conversation should be about the Bible and God but that all conversation should have a quality of grace, thoughtfulness, sensitivity, integrity, and respect for others. As for our resources, Professor Irv Brendlinger puts it clearly: "Wesley's perspective on material wealth was a simple matter of social concern, governed by love of neighbor and demonstrated by materially helping that neighbor."[5]

There should be no better citizen than a practicing Methodist. Social holiness means being ready to every good work. It thinks of service to others and practical concern for those in need—whatever the need—as a way of life to those who follow Jesus Christ. This is as simple as a casserole for the neighbor and as public as serving on the school board or the city council or beyond—and doing it all, not as a parading of piety but as an expression of the love of God as we have experienced it.

Christians should be experts in spiritual growth. We should be known not by our political affiliation or by any announced piety, but by a quality of life that is truly Christlike. If, as is now popularly said, people love Jesus but hate the church, then let church members solve the anomaly by being like Jesus Christ. Our contemporary culture seems, except for sports and money-grabbing, to be satisfied with mediocrity. Let the church lead the way into the excellence that matters most, without which all other achieving is meaningless: let us become pursuers and exemplars of holy character, beautiful inside and out.

Such a body of believers not only has a future, but it also promises a far better future for the times in which it lives. There is a wondrous spillover from such people, as even secular history has shown. It is not an easy solution; no true solution ever is. Its initial results may not produce impressive statistics. But this is a change that goes deep and high, and eventually will go far and wide.

So where does it begin? Methodism, in its several forms, has always had strong lay people. Not necessarily impressive by customary measure; at the first, in both England and America, quite the opposite. Such ordinary lay people were the day-by-day strength of the church. Sometimes, as in the magnificent story of William Wilberforce, deeply religious lay people turn the tide of history.[6] In The United Methodist Church, the most significant renewal movements have come through the Lay Witness Mission, the Emmaus Walk, and such study programs as DISCIPLE and *Christian Believer*.

But the primary burden of leadership falls on the clergy. Susanna Wesley urged son John in a letter in February 1726, to make a full examination of himself "that you may know whether you have a reasonable hope of salvation by Jesus Christ, that is, whether you are in a state of faith and repentance or not."[7] This was true for all believers, Susanna insisted, "but especially those designed for the clergy ought above all things to make their calling and election sure."[8] We ordained persons should listen hard to the Mother of Methodism. We should lead the way, expecting to be judged regularly on our work. And the examination and judgment should be more than a *pro forma* exercise.

What is true for clergy in general is especially true for those who appoint and oversee them, the bishops and district superintendents. These persons hold managerial responsibility, and they should be evaluated annually just as their counterparts are in industry, commerce, and sports. Perhaps it is time for the episcopacy to give up its lifetime status—a designation that makes bishops different from the rest of clergy—and be elected and re-elected at quadrennial or biquadrennial intervals. If lay and clergy are capable of electing bishops, then they should also be capable of judging their work and of assuming responsibility for such oversight. Such a provision would also make it possible for bishops to leave the post, if their hearts and spirits are so inclined, without feeling they have dishonored the office. Why should the episcopacy be seen as a lifetime act of the Spirit if the appointments of the other ordained clergy are not?

When one looks at the Methodist movement in its many expressions in 111 countries and its particular embodiment in The United Methodist Church, the third largest Christian body in the United States and still one of the more influential, one wonders if such a large and unwieldy ship can be turned around. Some will answer, perhaps in true piety and perhaps in an unholy cop out, "Only God knows."

I submit that what God knows is that God's people ought to be up and praying, up and believing, and up and doing and that God would be very pleased if we were. That's why I've thought it was worth my time to write this book and why I dare to think that it is worth your time to read it.

NOTES

1. How It All Began

1. John M. Todd, *John Wesley and the Catholic Church* (London: Hodder and Stoughton, 1958), 100.

2. Phyllis McGinley, *Saint-Watching* (New York: Viking Press, 1969), 216.

3. Todd, 192.

4. Halford E. Luccock and Paul Hutchinson, *The Story of Methodism* (Nashville: Abingdon-Cokesbury Press, 1926), 23-24.

2. A Village That Made a Difference

1. Maldwyn Edwards, *Family Circle* (London: Epworth Press, 1949, 1961), 60.

2. Ibid., 59.

3. Ibid., 62.

4. *The Oxford Dictionary of Quotations*, Sixth Edition, edited by Elizabeth Knowles (New York: Oxford University Press, 2004), 851.

5. Edwards, *Family Circle*, 66.

6. Ralph S. Cushman, *Practicing the Presence* (Nashville: Abingdon Press, 1936, 1964), 126.

7. Edwards, *Family Circle*, 31.

8. Ibid., 15.

9. Ibid., 21.

10. G. Elsie Harrison, *Son to Susanna* (Nashville: Cokesbury Press, 1938), 23.

11. Edwards, *Family Circle*, 27.

12. Halford E. Luccock and Paul Hutchinson, *The Story of Methodism* (Nashville: Abingdon-Cokesbury Press, 1926, 1949), 94.

13. Harrison, *Son to Susanna*, 50.

14. Edwards, *Family Circle*, 83.

3. How to Be Exclusively Inclusive

1. Philip S. Watson, *The Message of the Wesleys* (New York: The Macmillan Company, 1964), 39.

2. Excerpts from a sermon by John Wesley, "On Working Out Our Own Salvation," Sermon 90.

3. From *The Essential Works of John Wesley*, published, 1791, a section titled "Minutes of Several Conversations."

4. D. Michael Henderson, *John Wesley's Class Meeting* (Nappanee, IN: Evangel Publishing House, 1997), p. 84. Henderson is quoting from John Wesley, *Works*, VIII, 269.

5. http://www.qotd.org/search/search.html?aid=3881&page=3, p. 3 of a collection of John Wesley quotations.

6. John Wesley, "The Character of a Methodist," printed in pamphlet form by Discipleship Resources, Nashville.

4. A People of Head and Heart

1. Kenneth J. Collins, *John Wesley: A Theological Journey* (Nashville: Abingdon Press, 2003), 56.

2. Ibid., 56.

3. Ibid., 57.

4. G. Elsie Harrison, *Son to Susanna* (Nashville: Cokesbury Press, 1938), 176.

5. Ibid., 143.

6. Halford E. Luccock and Paul Hutchinson, *The Story of Methodism* (Nashville: Abingdon-Cokesbury Press, 1926, 1949), 70.

7. Collins, *John Wesley: A Theological Journey*, 87.

8. Luccock and Hutchinson, *The Story of Methodism*, 65.

9. J. Ellsworth Kalas, *Our First Song* (Nashville: Discipleship Resources, 1984; taken from the Asbury Seminary edition, 2007), 36-37.

5. What Methodists Believe

1. John Wesley, "The Character of a Methodist," printed in pamphlet form by Discipleship Resources, Nashville.

2. Ibid.

3. Henry Wheeler, *History and Exposition of the Twenty-five Articles of Religion of the Methodist Episcopal Church* (New York: Edaton & Mains; Cincinnati: Jennings & Graham, 1908), 9.

4. Ibid., 11.

5. John Wesley, "The Character of a Methodist."

6. Ibid.

7. Ibid.

8. Ibid.

9. Ibid.

10. Ibid.

11. Ibid.

12. Ibid.

13. Ibid.

14. Ibid.

15. Ibid.

16. Ibid.

6. A People Moving to Perfection

1. *The Random House Dictionary of the English Language*, Jess Stein, editor in chief (New York: Random House, 1966), 1079.

2. http://www.qotd.org/search/search.html?aid=3881&page=3, p. 3 of Wesley quotations.

3. William E. Sangster, *The Path to Perfection* (London: Epworth Press, 1943, 1984]), 154.

4. John Wesley, "A Plain Account of Christian Perfection" (London: Epworth Press, 1968), 26.

5. Irv Brendlinger, "Social Justice through the Eyes of Wesley," (Ontario: Sola Scriptura Ministries International, 2006), 108.

6. Philip S. Watson, *The Message of the Wesleys* (New York: The Macmillan Company, 1964), 204.

7. John Wesley, "A Plain Account of Christian Perfection," 111.

8. Ibid., 112.

9. Ibid., 34.

7. The Redeemed Person in an Unredeemed Society

1. Letter to Miss Furly, Sept 25, 1757.

2. Luccock and Hutchinson, *The Story of Methodism* (Nashville: Abingdon-Cokesbury Press, 1926, 1949), 121.

3. Philip Watson, *The Message of the Wesleys* (New York: The Macmillan Company, 1964), 57.

4. *The Works of John Wesley*, Third Edition, Vol. 5 (Grand Rapids: Baker Book House, 1979), 296.

5. Watson, *The Message of the Wesleys*, 57.

6. Ibid., 58.

7. Oscar Sherwin, *John Wesley, Friend of the People* (New York: Twayne Publishers, 1961), 125-26.

8. Ibid., 126.

9. Luccock and Hutchinson, *The Story of Methodism*, 192-93.

10. Ibid., 193.

11. Oscar Sherwin, *John Wesley, Friend of the People*, 107.

12. Ibid., 146.

13. John Wesley's letter to Wilberforce, quoted in Sherwin, *John Wesley, Friend of the People*, 177.

14. Ibid., 182.

15. Quoted in Sherwin, *John Wesley, Friend of the People*, 190.

16. Ibid.

8. Singing Like a Methodist

1. Elizabeth Knowles, editor, *Oxford Dictionary of Quotations*, Sixth Edition (New York: Oxford University Press, 2004), 326.

2. Fanny Crosby, "Redeemed," *The Hymnal for Worship and Celebration* (Waco, Texas: Word Music, 1986), no. 521.

3. G. Elsie Harrison, *Son to Susanna* (Nashville: Cokesbury Press, 1938), 116-17.

4. Ibid., 143.

5. *The United Methodist Hymnal* (Nashville: The United Methodist Publishing House, 1989), no. 342.

6. Ibid., 342.

7. Halford Luccock and Paul Hutchinson, *The Story of Methodism* (New York: Abingdon-Cokesbury Press, 1926), 105.

8. *Hymns for the Nativity of Our Lord* (London: William Strahan, 1745), 5.

9. Charles Wesley, "Arise, My Soul, Arise," *The Methodist Hymnal* (Nashville: The Methodist Publishing House, 1964, 1966), 122.

10. Luccock and Hutchinson, *The Story of Methodism*, 110-11.

11. *The United Methodist Hymnal*, no. 210.

12. J. Ellsworth Kalas, *Our First Song* (Nashville: Discipleship Resources, 1984; Asbury Seminary edition, 2007), 47.

13. Charles Wesley, "A Charge to Keep I Have," *The United Methodist Hymnal*, no. 413.

14. Charles Wesley, "O, for a Thousand Tongues to Sing," *The United Methodist Hymnal*, no. 57.

15. Charles Wesley, "A Charge to Keep I Have," *The United Methodist Hymnal*, no. 413.

16. J. Ellsworth Kalas, *Our First Song*, 2-3.

9. How Methodism Became America's Church

1. Halford E. Luccock and Paul Hutchinson, *The Story of Methodism* (Nashville: Abingdon-Cokesbury Press, 1926, 1949), 217.

2. John Wigger, *American Saint Francis Asbury and the Methodists* (New York: Oxford University Press, 2009), 90.

3. Ibid., 163.

4. Nathan O. Hatch, "The Puzzle of American Methodism," in *Methodism and the Shaping of American Culture*, Nathan O. Hatch and John H. Wigger, editors (Nashville: Kingswood Books, 2001), 27.

5. John Wesley, "Thoughts Upon Methodism," *The Works of the Reverend John Wesley, A. M.* (J. Emory and B. Waugh, for the Methodist Episcoipal Church, 1831), 315.

6. Robert D. Clark, "The Life of Matthew Simpson" (New York: The Macmillan Company, 1956), vii.

7. Ibid., 235.

8. Jeffrey Simpson, *Chautauqua: An American Utopia* (New York: Harry N. Abrams, Inc., 1999), 45.

9. *Bartlett's Familiar Quotations*, Seventeenth Edition, Justin Kaplan, general editor (New York: Little, Brown and Company, 2003), 319.

10. Methodism and Her Several Children

1. Halford E. Luccock and Paul Hutchinson, *The Story of Methodism* (Nashville: Abingdon-Cokesbury Press, 1926, 1949), 196.

2. Ibid., 200.

3. National statistics are from the "District Statistician's Report to the General Secretary for Fiscal Year Ending August 31, 2011," from the official Wesleyan Church website. The worldwide statistic is from "The Wesleyan Church World Summary of General Statistics for Fiscal Year Ending August 31, 2010."

4. Abraham Lincoln, "Second Inaugural Address," *A Treasury of the Familiar*, edited by Ralph L. Woods (New York: The Macmillan Company, 1945), 171.

12. What Is the Future of Methodism?

1. Rudyard Kipling, "Recessional," from *A Treasure of the Familiar*, edited by Ralph L. Woods (New York: The Macmillan Company, 1945), 594-95.

2. "Thoughts Upon Methodism," *The Works of the Reverend John Wesley*, A. M. (J. Emory and B. Waugh, for the Methodist Episcopal Church, 1831), 315.

3. Halford E. Luccock and Paul Hutchins, *The Story of Methodism* (Nashville: Abingdon-Cokesbury Press, 1926, 1949), 110.

4. *The United Methodist Hymnal* (Nashville: The United Methodist Publishing House, 1989), no. 342.

5. Irv Brendlinger, *Social Justice through the Eyes of Wesley* (Kitchener, Canada: Sola Scriptura Ministries International, 2006), 121.

6. I urge you to read the Wilberforce story in the inspiring biography by Eric Metaxas, *Amazing Grace* (New York: HarperCollins, 2009).

7. Kenneth J. Collins, *John Wesley, a Theological Journey* (Nashville: Abingdon Press, 2003), 29-30.

8. Ibid.

DISCUSSION GUIDE

Chapter 1: How It All Began

1. Before beginning this book, what does/did it mean for you to "be United Methodist"? What are your perceptions of the denomination and who we are as a people?
2. Most Protestant denominations got their start by splitting with another group over a specific issue: Lutherans over indulgences, Anglicans over Henry VIII's divorce, Pentecostals over how the Holy Spirit works, and so on. But the "birth" of Methodism is a little harder to pin down. Is this an advantage or a disadvantage for the Methodist movement? Why or why not?
3. The author points out that one of the early points of origin for Methodism, Wesley's Aldersgate experience, happened when an *Anglican* priest was listening to the reading of a *Lutheran* document while attending a *Moravian* gathering. In your experience or view of United Methodism today, do United Methodists still draw from a variety of influences and traditions? Explain your answer in some detail.
4. Methodism took hold in England and America because there was a "market" for what it offered. What is the religious "marketplace" like where you live? What are its needs? Do you

think The United Methodist Church meets the needs of that market? Why or why not? In what ways might the UMC improve in this regard?

5. In Wesley's time there was a lot of corruption in the church, and many people felt a deep cynicism toward it. Do you see similarities and/or differences between the way the church was perceived in the eighteenth century and today? Explain your answer, and give some examples.

6. Do you agree with the author's assertion that in our own time "we have lost our moral moorings because our generation is no longer sure that there is a moral compass"? Why or why not?

7. Do you think that United Methodism can be part of a revival of faith in the twenty-first century the way Methodism was in the eighteenth? Give reasons for your answer.

Chapter 2: A Village That Made a Difference

1. Modern psychology tells us that our earliest experiences with our parents play a huge role in shaping our personalities, and the Wesley family is proof of this. What did you notice in this chapter about John and Charles that was shaped by their parents?

2. Think about your own upbringing. In what ways, positive or negative, did your parents shape who you are? Did your family have anything in common with the Wesley family? How was your family similar to or different from the Wesleys?

3. To say that Susanna Wesley was a strict parent is to put it mildly. Do you think such rigid structure is a good thing? Why or why not?

4. Samuel Wesley was a scholar as well as a pastor, because at the time, a clergyperson was expected to be one of the most educated people in the community. Are the perceptions and expectations of clergy different today than in Wesley's time? If so, how?

5. John Wesley's early experience of nearly dying in a fire, being "a brand plucked from the burning," clearly had a huge influence on the rest of his life. Have you or has anyone you know had an experience that, in hindsight, formed your understanding of who you are and the purpose of your life? What did that experience involve, or what might such an experience look and feel like?

6. Susanna Wesley's influence led her son John to be ahead of his time in his attitude toward women's leadership in the church. In your experience, does The United Methodist Church carry on this broadly inclusive tradition? Why or why not?

Chapter 3: How to Be Exclusively Inclusive

1. What do the words *inclusive* and *exclusive* mean to you?

2. There is an inherent tension in being a disciple of Jesus—you are welcome as you are, but you are not welcome to stay that way. How do you experience this tension in your own journey of discipleship?

3. Methodism began as a "movement" and not a "church" because the Methodists met people where they were and didn't wait for the masses to come to them. Do you see this happening in The United Methodist Church of today? If so, how? If not, how could we be doing this in our own contexts?

4. John Wesley cared more for the condition of the souls under his care than he did the raw numbers. Do you think the church of today has maintained this focus? Why or why not?

5. In reading the description of the early Methodist societies, what stands out to you? Do you see similarities and/or differences between the societies and your own Sunday school class or other small group? Give some examples.

6. John Wesley's discipline was extremely rigid, which we might find off-putting or even offensive today. But the early Methodists found these high standards invigorating, not discouraging. Why do you think this is?

7. Is there a place for "class meetings" in our own day and time? Why or why not? How might they be similar to or different from the class meetings of Wesley's day?

8. Do you agree with the author's assertion that people are as "God hungry" today as they ever have been? If so, how do people express that hunger?

Chapter 4: A People of Head and Heart

1. Is your experience of faith more head oriented or heart oriented? Why do you think that is?

2. If you're a "head" person, do you find it difficult to engage your heart in your faith? If you're a "heart" person, do you find it difficult to engage your head in your faith? Why or why not?

3. Do you think The United Methodist Church of today leans more toward the head or the heart? Why do you think this is? Are we going in the right direction, or could we benefit from a bigger dose of the other?

4. John Wesley finally began to engage his heart in his faith when he experienced a crisis. Have you ever had a crisis or tough experience in your life that affected your faith in some way? What was that like?

5. How do you go about balancing your emotions and your intellect in your faith?

Chapter 5: What Methodists Believe

1. Before beginning this chapter, what was your perception of what the core beliefs of United Methodism are? Did reading this chapter change your perception? If so, how?

2. Like the last chapter's focus on head and heart, this chapter focuses on a healthy balance of belief and practice. In your own faith life, do you tend to emphasize belief or practice more? Why?

3. Wesley wrote, as to opinions which do not strike at the root of real Christianity, "we think and let think." This assumes, of course, that we all agree on what the root of real Christianity is. What do you believe is the "root of real Christianity"? What are the absolute essential things that make one a Christian?

4. Wesley, and the Methodist tradition that follows him, holds that the Bible is "the only and sufficient rule of Christian faith and practice." How do you understand this statement?

5. The author argues that we have to submit ourselves to the authority of Scripture and not try to accommodate it to our prejudices or presuppositions. How do we know the difference?

6. If we have no real doctrinal differences with the Anglican Church (the Episcopal Church in the United States), do you think that United Methodism should be its own separate denomination? Why or why not?

7. Wesley was most interested in the "fruit" in the lives of Methodists. He wanted doctrinal beliefs to lead to some sort of tangible difference. What do you think is the most important "fruit" in the life of a Christian?

Chapter 6: A People Moving to Perfection

1. *Perfect* is clearly a loaded word. What does perfect mean to you?

2. Do you think that taking satisfaction in doing something good makes you self-righteous? In other words, does thinking that you are a good person make you a bad person? Explain.

3. Can you be perfect and still make mistakes? Why or why not?

4. Practicing the love of God toward our neighbor means that we somehow see God in everyone. Do you know anyone in whom it is hard to see God? What makes seeing God in someone like this so hard?

5. Have you ever found yourself at a point or points where you say to yourself, *I have arrived*? What was that like? How long did it last before you were reminded that you were not, in fact, perfect?

6. According to Wesley's understanding of Christian perfection, the motivation behind our actions is the key to knowing whether we're on the right track. How do we go about discerning what our true motivation is?

Chapter 7: The Redeemed Person in an Unredeemed Society

1. What do you make of the idea that the poor are poor because they want to be, or that their condition is somehow their fault?

2. What are your thoughts on the idea that the church's job is to reform the nation? What does that look like in our own day and time?

3. John and Charles Wesley believed that personal piety and social holiness were inseparable, but in the times in which we live, they seem like polar opposites. What might the fusion of personal and social holiness look like in your own context?

4. Is it possible to critique specific behaviors without being judgmental? If so, how does that work?

5. After reading this chapter and seeing Wesley's stand on different social and cultural issues, how do you think he would fit into the liberal/conservative camps of our own time?

6. In America, Methodism's emphasis on social holiness became diluted as it gained prominence and respectability in the society (something it had little of in Wesley's time). How do you think the temptations of social prominence persuade us to stay silent on important social issues now?

7. Do you think that The United Methodist Church takes social holiness seriously? Why or why not?

Chapter 8: Singing Like a Methodist

1. What role do songs and singing play in your own faith? Does it surprise you that songs were such a big deal in early Methodism? Why or why not?
2. Songs took on a somewhat different character in societies where many people couldn't read. Try to recall a few key sentences from the last sermon you heard. Now try to remember the chorus from the last song you heard. Which is easier? Does this give you a better sense of what singing meant to earlier cultures, particularly the early Methodists? If so, how?
3. When asked, "What is your favorite hymn?" what immediately comes to mind? What is it about that particular hymn that stands out? How does that hymn shape your faith?
4. Are there particular songs that comfort you in times of uncertainty or distress (religious or otherwise)? What is it about these songs that is comforting to you?
5. What do you make of Andrew Fletcher's assertion that "the ballads people sing do more to shape the world than the laws the legislatures pass"? Do you agree or disagree? Why?

Chapter 9: How Methodism Became America's Church

1. Methodism spread across the United States of America because of circuit-riding bachelor preachers. Would a similar model work in the U.S. today? Why or why not? What would be the most effective method for spreading the faith today?
2. As Methodism grew, it gained more political influence. Is it a good thing for religious leaders to have a lot of interaction and influence with political leaders? Why or why not?
3. Education and cultural learning played a big role in Methodist history. Do you think that the church should still be involved in education today? Why or why not?
4. The history of Methodism and the history of the United States are closely intertwined, their changes often paralleling

one another. What sorts of changes do you see happening in the United States today? How should The United Methodist Church respond to these changes?

Chapter 10: Methodism and Her Several Children

1. What are some of the benefits to religious groups splitting away and becoming independent of one another? What are the drawbacks?
2. The first big split in American Methodism was the result of a conflict over how much power the bishops and clergy had compared to that of the laypeople. How much of a say should laypeople have in how the church is run?
3. Because of the mergers of the twentieth century, The United Methodist Church is a large and diverse body. What do you see as the good and the bad points of having such a "big tent"?
4. What does the knowledge that Methodism "gave birth" to groups as diverse as the Salvation Army, Pentecostalism, and the Nazarene Church say to you about the future of The United Methodist Church? Do you think it would be beneficial for us to "give birth" to more new movements and bodies? Why or why not?

Chapter 11: Methodism Today

1. Before reading this chapter, what was your perception of the state of Methodism today? Did anything in this chapter change that perception? If so, what?
2. Do you agree with the author's assertion that "there is little reason to remain a Methodist and still less reason to encourage others to become Methodists if one knows nothing about the church and its teachings that give one reason for worthy pride and for the difference that Methodism might bring to everyday life"? Why or why not? What importance does our history and doctrine play in defining who we are today?

3. The author identifies disagreements over sexual orientation as one of the chief ways we are "divided and distracted." What other issues do you see driving the church today, either in your congregation, conference, or the entire denomination?
4. What unites the church? What common understandings and commitments hold us together throughout all the division we see around us?
5. What would you say is the "identity" of The United Methodist Church?

Chapter 12: What Is the Future of Methodism?

1. How do you react when you hear people say that they are "spiritual but not religious" or that they "like Jesus but not the church"? Are these valid statements? Why or why not?
2. What does the statistical decline of The United Methodist Church and other Protestant denominations say about the current state and the future of them?
3. Before beginning this book, what was your general impression of United Methodism? Who did you think United Methodists are? What did you think they believed? Has anything in this book changed those perceptions? If so, what?
4. What do you believe is the future of The United Methodist Church? What role do you see yourself and your congregation playing in this future?

CPSIA information can be obtained
at www.ICGtesting.com
Printed in the USA
LVHW090952170619
621453LV00001B/64/P